The everyday world at your fingertips

Italian
picture dictionary

www.berlitzpublishing.com

Distribution

UK, Ireland and Europe:
Apa Publications (UK) Ltd;
sales@insightguides.com
United States and Canada:
Ingram Publisher Services;
ips@ingramcontent.com
Australia and New Zealand:
Woodslane; info@woodslane.com.au
Southeast Asia:
Apa Publications (SN) Pte;
singaporeoffice@insightguides.com
Hong Kong, Taiwan and China:
Apa Publications (HK) Ltd;
hongkongoffice@insightguides.com
Worldwide: Apa Publications (UK) Ltd;
sales@insightguides.com

**Special Sales, Content Licensing
and CoPublishing**

Insight Guides can be purchased in bulk
quantities at discounted prices. We can
create special editions, personalised
jackets and corporate imprints tailored to
your needs. sales@insightguides.com;
www.insightguides.biz

First Edition 2017

Contact us

Every effort has been made to provide
accurate information in this publication
but changes are inevitable. The publisher
cannot be responsible for any resulting
loss, inconvenience or injury. We would
appreciate it if readers would call our
attention to any errors or outdated
information. We also welcome your
suggestions; please contact us at:
berlitz@apaguide.co.uk

Berlitz Trademark Reg. U.S. Patent Office
and other countries. Marca Registrada.
Used under licence from the Berlitz
Investment Corporation

Series Editor: Carine Tracanelli
Editor: Berenika Wilczyńska
Head of Production: Rebeka Davies
Series design: Krzysztof Kop
Picture research & DTP design:
Tamkapress
English text: Carine Tracanelli &
Barbara Marchwica

Introduction

Whether you are a total beginner or already have a sound knowledge of your chosen language, this Berlitz picture dictionary will help you to communicate quickly and easily. Packed with 2,000 useful terms, it covers all everyday situations, whether you're applying for a job, going shopping or just getting around. See, understand, memorise: visual learning by combining a word with an image helps you remember it more effectively as images affect us more than text alone.

To get the most out of your picture dictionary you can search for words in two ways: by theme (women's clothes, sporting facilities, hobbies, etc.) or by consulting the index at the end. You'll also find important phrases surrounding a topic in each chapter, ensuring that you have the foundations you need for communicating.

Each word is followed by its phonetic transcription to make sure you pronounce each word or sentence correctly. You will find a helpful guide to pronunciation in your chosen language on pages 7–10.

Note that the terms in this picture dictionary are always given in their singular form unless they are generally only used in their plural form, and all nouns are preceded by their gender-specific article. Certain terms are not gender-neutral and in such cases all genders are provided throughout in both the translation and phonetic transcription, ensuring you can communicate in all variants.

Berlitz are renowned for the quality and expertise of their language products. Discover the full range at www.berlitzpublishing.com.

Table of Contents

Pronunciation

This section is designed to make you familiar with the sounds of Italian using our simplified phonetic transcription. You'll find the pronunciation of the Italian letters and sounds explained below, together with their "imitated" equivalents. This system is used throughout the picture dictionary; simply read the pronunciation as if it were English, noting any special rules below.

Stress has been indicated in the phonetic pronunciations by capital letters. These letters should be pronounced with more emphasis. Generally, the vowel of the next to last syllable is stressed. When a final vowel is stressed, it has an accent mark, i.e. è, ì.

PRONUNCIATION

Consonants

Letter(s)	Approximate Pronunciation	Symbol	Example	Pronunciation
c	1. before e and i, like ch in *chip*	ch	**cerco**	CHEHR-koh
	2. elsewhere, like c in *cat*	k	**conto**	KOHN-toh
ch	like c in *cat*	k	**che**	keh
g	1. before e and i, like j in *jet*	j	**valigia**	vah-LEE-jah
	2. elsewhere, like g in *go*	g	**grande**	GRAHN-deh
gh	g like g in *go*	gh	**laghi**	LAH-ghee
gli	lli like in *million*	ly	**bagaglio**	bah-GAH-llyoh
gn	ni like in *onion*	ny	**bagno**	BAH-nyoh
h	always silent		**ha**	ah
r	rolled in the back of the mouth	r	**Roma**	ROH-mah
s	1. generally like s in *sit*	s	**salsa**	SAHL-sah
	2. between two vowels and before b, d, g, l, m, n, r, v like z in *zoo*	z	**casa**	KAH-zah
sc	1. before e and i, like sh in *shut*	sh	**uscita**	oo-SHEE-tah
	2. elsewhere, like sk in *skin*	sk	**scarpa**	SKAHR-pah
sch	like sk in *skin*	sk	**scherzo**	SKEHR-tsoh
z	1. generally ts as in *hits*	ts	**grazie**	GRAH-tsyeh
	2. sometimes (i.e. initially) a little softer, like dz	ts	**zero**	DZEH-roh

The letters b, d, f, k, l, m, n, p, q, t and v are pronounced approximately as in English. The letters j, k, w, x and y are not true members of the Italian alphabet and appear only in foreign words or names. All consonants (except for h) can be doubled, i.e. *carro*, *mazzo*, *passare*. They are pronounced as doubled letters (more intensely).

Vowels

Letter	Approximate Pronunciation	Symbol	Example	Pronunciation
a	short, like a in *father*	ah	**gatto**	GAHT-toh
e	like e in *get* or in *they* (but without the final i)	eh	**destra**	DEH-strah
i	like ee in *meet*	ee	**vini**	VEE-nee
o	like o in *so*	oh	**sole**	SOH-leh
u	like oo in *boot*	oo	**fumo**	FOO-moh

Vowel Combinations

Letters	Symbol	Example	Pronunciation
ae	ah-EH	**paese**	pah-EH-zeh
ao	AH-oh	**Paolo**	PAH-oh-loh
au	ow	**auto**	OW-toh
eo	EH-oh	**museo**	moo-ZEH-oh
eu	ehw	**euro**	EHW-roh
ei	ay	**lei**	lay

Letters	Symbol	Example	Pronunciation
ia	yah	**piazza**	PYAH-tstsah
ie	yeh	**piede**	PYEH-deh
io	yoh	**piove**	PYOH-veh
iu	yoo	**più**	pyoo
oa	OH-ah	**oasi**	OH-ah-zee
oe	oh-EH	**poeta**	poh-EH-tah
oi	oy	**puoi**	pwoy
ua	wah	**quale**	KWAH-leh
ue	weh	**questo**	KWEH-stoh
ui	wee	**qui**	kwee
uo	woh	**può**	pwoh

A B C D E F G H I J K L M N
O P Q R S T U V W X Y Z

GENERAL VOCABULARY

first name
nome
NOH-meh

date of birth
data di nascita
DAH-tah dee NA-shee-tah

place of birth
luogo di nascita
LWOH-goh dee NA-shee-tah

email address
indirizzo email
een-dee-REE-tstsoh ee-MAYL

phone number
numero di telefono
NOO-meh-roh dee teh-LEH-foh-noh

last name
cognome
koh-NYOH-meh

age
età
eh-TAH

address	**indirizzo**	een-dee-REE-tstsoh
marital status	**stato civile**	STAH-toh chee-VEE-leh
children	**bambini**	bahm-BEE-nee
home country	**paese natale**	pah-EH-zeh nah-TAH-eh
place of residence	**residenza**	reh-zee-DEHN-tsah
single	**celibe / nubile**	CHEH-lee-beh / NOO-bee-leh
in a relationship	**in una relazione**	een OO-nah reh-lah-TSYOH-neh
divorced	**divorziato / divorziata**	dee-vohr-TSYAH-toh / dee-vohr-TSYAH-tah
married	**sposato / sposata**	spoh-ZAH-toh / spoh-ZAH-tah
widowed	**vedovo / vedova**	VEH-doh-voh / VEH-doh-vah
What's your name?	**Qual è il tuo nome?**	kwah-LEH eel TOO-oh NOH-meh?
Where are you from?	**Di dove sei?**	dee DOH-veh say?
Where were you born?	**Dove sei nato / nata?**	DOH-veh say NAH-toh / NAH-tah?
When were you born?	**Quando sei nato / nata?**	KWAN-doh say NAH-toh / NAH-tah?
What is your address?	**Qual è il tuo indirizzo?**	kwah-LEH eel TOO-oh een-dee-REE-tstsoh?
What's your phone number?	**Qual è il tuo numero di telefono?**	kwah-LEH eel TOO-oh NOO-meh-roh dee teh-LEH-foh-noh?
Are you married?	**Sei sposato / sposata?**	say spoh-ZAH-toh / spoh-ZAH-tah?
Do you have children?	**Hai figli?**	ahy FEE-lly?

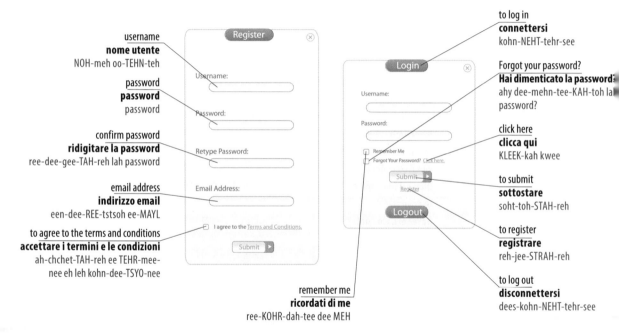

username
nome utente
NOH-meh oo-TEHN-teh

password
password
password

confirm password
ridigitare la password
ree-dee-gee-TAH-reh lah password

email address
indirizzo email
een-dee-REE-tstsoh ee-MAYL

to agree to the terms and conditions
accettare i termini e le condizioni
ah-chchet-TAH-reh ee TEHR-mee-nee eh leh kohn-dee-TSYO-nee

to log in
connettersi
kohn-NEHT-tehr-see

Forgot your password?
Hai dimenticato la password?
ahy dee-mehn-tee-KAH-toh la password?

click here
clicca qui
KLEEK-kah kwee

to submit
sottostare
soht-toh-STAH-reh

to register
registrare
reh-jee-STRAH-reh

to log out
disconnettersi
dees-kohn-NEHT-tehr-see

remember me
ricordati di me
ree-KOHR-dah-tee dee MEH

0 1 2 3 4 5 6 7 8 9

0	zero	**zero**	DZEH-roh
1	one	**uno**	OO-noh
2	two	**due**	DOO-weh
3	three	**tre**	treh
4	four	**quattro**	KWAT-troh
5	five	**cinque**	CHEEN-kweh
6	six	**sei**	say
7	seven	**sette**	SEHT-teh
8	eight	**otto**	OHT-toh
9	nine	**nove**	NOH-veh
10	ten	**dieci**	DYEH-chee
11	eleven	**undici**	UHN-dee-chee
12	twelve	**dodici**	DOH-dee-chee
13	thirteen	**tredici**	TREH-dee-chee
14	fourteen	**quattordici**	kwaht-TOR-dee-chee
15	fifteen	**quindici**	KWEEN-dee-chee
16	sixteen	**sedici**	SEH-dee-chee

17	seventeen	**diciassette**	dee-chyahs-SEHT-teh
18	eighteen	**diciotto**	dee-CHYOHT-toh
19	nineteen	**diciannove**	dee-chyahn-NOH-veh
20	twenty	**venti**	VEHN-tee
21	twenty-one	**ventuno**	vehn-TOO-noh
30	thirty	**trenta**	TREHN-tah
40	forty	**quaranta**	kwah-RAHN-tah
50	fifty	**cinquanta**	cheen-KWAHN-tah
60	sixty	**sessanta**	sehs-SAHN-tah
70	seventy	**settanta**	seht-TAHN-tah
80	eighty	**ottanta**	oht-TAHN-tah
90	ninety	**novanta**	noh-VAHN-tah
100	one hundred	**cento**	CHEHN-toh
101	one hundred and one	**centouno**	chehn-toh-OO-noh
1000	one thousand	**mille**	MEEL-leh
1 000 000	one million	**milione**	meel-YOH-neh

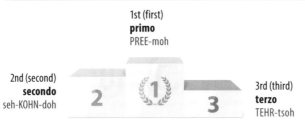

1st (first)
primo
PREE-moh

2nd (second)
secondo
seh-KOHN-doh

3rd (third)
terzo
TEHR-tsoh

4th	fourth	**quarto**	KWAHR-toh	21st	twenty-first	**ventunesimo**	vehn-too-NEH-zee-moh
5th	fifth	**quinto**	KWEEN-toh	22nd	twenty-second	**ventiduesimo**	vehn-tee-doo-WEH-zee-moh
6th	sixth	**sesto**	SEHS-toh	23rd	twenty-third	**ventitreesimo**	vehn-tee-treh-EH-zee-moh
7th	seventh	**settimo**	SEHT-tee-moh	24th	twenty-fourth	**ventiquattresimo**	vehn-tee-kwaht-TREH-zee-moh
8th	eighth	**ottavo**	oht-TAH-voh	25th	twenty-fifth	**venticinquesimo**	vehn-tee-cheen-KWEH-zee-moh
9th	ninth	**nono**	NOH-noh	26th	twenty-sixth	**ventiseiesimo**	vehn-tee-seh-YEH-zee-moh
10th	tenth	**decimo**	DEH-chee-moh	27th	twenty-seventh	**ventisettesimo**	vehn-tee-seht-TEH-zee-moh
11th	eleventh	**undicesimo**	oon-dee-CHEH-zee-moh	28th	twenty-eighth	**ventottesimo**	vehn-toht-TEH-zee-moh
12th	twelfth	**dodicesimo**	doh-dee-CHEH-zee-moh	29th	twenty-ninth	**ventinovesimo**	vehn-tee-noh-WEH-zee-moh
13th	thirteenth	**tredicesimo**	treh-dee-CHEH-zee-moh	30th	thirtieth	**trentesimo**	tren-TEH-zee-moh
14th	fourteenth	**quattordicesimo**	kwaht-tor-dee-CHEH-zee-moh	40th	fortieth	**quarantesimo**	kwah-rahn-TEH-zee-moh
15th	fifteenth	**quindicesimo**	kween-dee-CHEH-zee-moh	50th	fiftieth	**cinquantesimo**	cheen-kwahn-TEH-zee-moh
16th	sixteenth	**sedicesimo**	seh-dee-CHEH-zee-moh	60th	sixtieth	**sessantesimo**	sehs-sahn-TEH-zee-moh
17th	seventeenth	**diciassettesimo**	dee-chyas-seht-TEH-zee-moh	70th	seventieth	**settantesimo**	seht-tahn-TEH-zee-moh
18th	eighteenth	**diciottesimo**	dee-chyoht-TEH-zee-moh	80th	eightieth	**ottantesimo**	oht-tahn-TEH-zee-moh
19th	nineteenth	**diciannovesimo**	doo-chyahn-noh-VEH-zee-moh	90th	ninetieth	**novantesimo**	noh-vahn-TEH-zee-moh
20th	twentieth	**ventesimo**	vehn-TEH-zee-moh	100th	hundredth	**centesimo**	chehn-TEH-zee-moh

noon	**mezzogiorno**	meh-tstsoh-JYOHR-noh
midnight	**mezzanotte**	meh-dzdzah-NOHT-teh

one am	**l'una**	LOO-nah
one pm	**le tredici**	leh TREH-dee-chee

two am	**le due**	leh DOO-weh
two pm	**le quattordici**	leh kwaht-TOHR-dee-chee

three am	**le tre**	leh treh
three pm	**le quindici**	leh KWEEN-dee-chee

four am	**le quattro**	leh KWAHT-troh
four pm	**le sedici**	leh SEH-dee-chee

five am	**le cinque**	leh CHEEN-kweh
five pm	**le diciassette**	leh dee-chyahs-SEHT-teh

six am	**le sei**	leh say
six pm	**le diciotto**	leh dee-CHYOHT-toh

seven am	**le sette**	leh SEHT-teh
seven pm	**le diciannove**	leh dee-chyahn-NOH-veh

eight am	**le otto**	leh OHT-toh
eight pm	**le venti**	leh VEHN-tee

nine am	**le nove**	leh NOH-veh
nine pm	**le ventuno**	leh vehn-TOO-noh

ten am	**le dieci**	leh DYEH-chee
ten pm	**le ventidue**	leh vehn-tee-DOO-weh

eleven am	**le undici**	leh OON-dee-chee
eleven pm	**le ventitré**	leh vehn-tee-TREH

quarter to
... meno un quarto
... MEH-noh oon KWAHR-toh

ten to
... meno dieci
... MEH-noh DYEH-chee

five to
... meno cinque
... MEH-noh CHEEN-kweh

... o'clock
l'ora
LOH-rah

five past
... e cinque
... eh CHEEN-kweh

ten past
... e dieci
... eh DYEH-chee

quarter past
... e un quarto
... eh oon KWAHR-toh

half past
... e mezza
... eh MEH-dzdzah

What time is it?	**Che ore sono?**	keh OH-reh SOH-noh?
It's nine thirty.	**Sono le nove e trenta.**	SOH-noh leh NOH-veh eh TREHN-tah.
Excuse me, could you tell me the time please?	**Scusa, puoi dirmi che ore sono?**	SKOO-zah, pwoy DEER-mee keh OH-reh SOH-noh?
It's about half past nine.	**Sono circa le nove e mezza.**	SOH-noh CHEER-kah leh NOH-veh eh MEH-dzdzah.

Monday
lunedì
loo-neh-DEE

Tuesday
martedì
mahr-teh-DEE

Wednesday
mercoledì
mehr-koh-leh-DEE

Thursday
giovedì
jyoh-veh-DEE

Friday
venerdì
veh-nehr-DEE

Saturday
sabato
SAH-bah-toh

Sunday
domenica
doh-MEH-nee-kah

on Monday	**lunedì**	loo-neh-DEE
from Tuesday	**da martedì**	dah mahr-teh-DEE
until Wednesday	**fino a mercoledì**	FEE-noh ah mehr-koh-leh-DEE

JANUARY

January
gennaio
jehn-NAH-yoh

FEBRUARY

February
febbraio
fehb-BRAH-yoh

MARCH

March
marzo
MAHR-tsoh

APRIL

April
aprile
ah-PREE-leh

MAY

May
maggio
MAH-djdjoh

JUNE

June
giugno
JYOO-nyoh

JULY

July
luglio
LOOL-yoh

AUGUST

August
agosto
ah-GOH-stoh

SEPTEMBER

September
settembre
seht-TEHM-breh

OCTOBER

October
ottobre
oht-TOH-breh

NOVEMBER

November
novembre
noh-VEHM-breh

DECEMBER

December
dicembre
dee-CHEHM-breh

in July	**in luglio**	een LOOL-yoh
since September	**da settembre**	dah seht-TEHM-breh
until October	**fino a ottobre**	FEE-noh ah oht-TOH-breh
for two months	**per due mesi**	pehr DOO-weh MEH-zee

morning	late morning	noon	afternoon	evening	night
il mattino	**prima di mezzogiorno**	**il mezzogiorno**	**il pomeriggio**	**la sera**	**la notte**
eel maht-TEE-noh	PREE-mah dee meh-dzdzoh-JYOHR-noh	eel meh-dzdzoh-JYOHR-noh	eel poh-meh-REE-djdjyoh	lah SEH-rah	lah NOHT-teh

in the morning	**di mattina**	dee maht-TEE-nah
in the evening	**di sera**	dee SEH-rah
in the night	**di notte**	dee NOHT-teh

cash
contanti
kohn-TAHN-tee

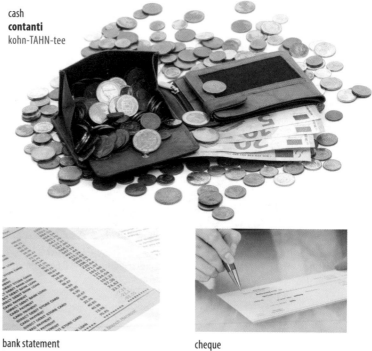

ATM / cashpoint
il bancomat
eel BAHN-koh-maht

bank statement
l'estratto conto
leh-STRAHT-toh KOHN-toh

cheque
l'assegno
lahs-SEH-nyoh

account	**il conto bancario**	eel KOHN-toh bahn-KHAR-yoh
bank	**la banca**	lah BAHN-kah
bank charges	**le spese bancarie**	leh SPEH-zeh bahn-KAHR-yeh
debit card	**la carta di debito**	lah KAHR-tah dee DEH-bee-toh
debt	**il debito**	eel DEH-bee-toh
current account	**il conto corrente**	eel KOHN-toh kohr-REHN-teh
loan	**il prestito**	eel PREHS-tee-toh
mortgage	**il mutuo**	eel MOO-too-woh
savings account	**il conto di risparmio**	eel KOHN-toh dee rees-PAHR-myoh
standing order	**il prelievo automatico**	eel preh-LYE-voh ow-toh-MAH-tee-koh
to borrow money	**prendere in prestito denaro**	PREHN-deh-reh een PREHS-tee-toh deh-NAH-roh
to invest	**investire**	een-vehs-TEE-reh
to lend money	**prestare denaro**	preh-STAH-reh deh-NAH-roh
to pay	**pagare**	pah-GAH-reh
to take out a loan	**prendere un prestito**	PREHN-deh-reh oon PREHS-tee-toh
to withdraw from the account	**prelevare dal conto**	preh-leh-VAH-reh dahl KOHN-toh
to take out a mortgage	**accendere un mutuo**	ah-CHCHEHN-deh-reh oon MOO-too-woh
to withdraw	**prelevare**	preh-leh-VAH-reh

credit card
la carta di credito
lah KAHR-tah dee KREH-dee-toh

to save
risparmiare
rees-pahr-MYAH-reh

Pound Sterling
lira sterlina
LEE-rah stehr-LEE-nah

Euro
euro
EHW-roh

Dollar
dollaro
DOHL-lah-roh

Franc
franco
FRAHN-koh

Yen
yen
yehn

Won
won
vahn

Yuan
yuan
YOO-ahn

Indian Rupee
rupia indiana
ROO-pyah een-DYAH-nah

Zloty
zloty
ZLOH-tee

Ruble
rublo
ROO-bloh

Leu
leu
lehw

Forint
fiorino
fyoh-REE-noh

Krone	corona	koh-ROH-nah
Peso	peso	PEH-zoh
Pound	sterlina	stehr-LEE-nah
Dinar	dinaro	DEE-nah-roh
Shilling	scellino	shehl-LEE-noh
Dirham	dirham	DEE-rahm
Rial	rial	ryahl
Dong	dong	dohng

exchange rate	il tasso di cambio	eel TAHS-soh dee KAHM-byoh
exchange rate for US Dollars to Japanese Yen	il tasso di cambio di dollari per yen giapponese	eel TAHS-soh dee KAHM-byoh dee DOHL-lah-ree pehr yehn jyahp-poh-NEH-zeh
foreign exchange	il cambio	eel KAHM-byoh
foreign exchange rate	il tasso di cambio	eel TAHS-soh dee KAHM-byoh

 PEOPLE

a middle-aged man
l'uomo di mezza età
LWOH-moh dee MEH-dzdzah eh-TAH

an old man
l'uomo anziano
LWOH-moh ahn-TSYAH-noh

a young woman
la donna giovane
lah DOHN-nah JYOH-vah-neh

baby
il bimbo
eel BEEM-boh

a young man
il giovane
eel JYOH-vah-neh

a teenage boy
il ragazzo
eel rah-GAH-tstsoh

a teenage girl
la ragazza
lah rah-GAH-tstsah

a young boy
il bambino
eel bahm-BEE-noh

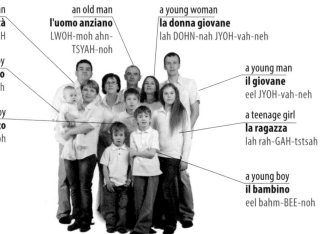

child	**il bambino**	eel bahm-BEE-noh	old	**vecchio**	VEHK-kyoh
teenager	**l'adolescente**	lah-doh-leh-SHEHN-teh	adult	**adulto**	ah-DOOL-toh
a young girl	**la bambina**	lah bahm-BEE-nah	She is forty years old.	**Lei ha quarant'anni.**	lay ah KWAH-rahn-tahn-nee
a seven-year-old girl	**la bambina di sette anni**	lah bahm-BEE-nah dee SEHT-teh AHN-nee	She is in her thirties.	**Lei è una trentenne.**	lay EH oo-nah trehnt-EHN-neh
young	**giovane**	JYOH-vah-neh	She is about twenty.	**Lei ha circa vent'anni.**	lay ah CHEER-kah vehnt-AHN-nee
a little boy	**il ragazzino**	eel rah-GAH-tstsee-noh	He is six years old.	**Lui ha sei anni.**	LOO-yee ah say AHN-nee
a little girl	**la ragazzina**	lah rah-GAH-tstsee-nah			
middle-aged	**di mezza età**	dee MEH-dzdzah eh-TAH			

a beautiful girl
una bella ragazza
OO-nah BEHL-lah rah-GAH-tstsah

a pretty woman
una donna graziosa
OO-nah DOHN-nah grah-TSYOH-zah

a handsome man
un bell'uomo
oon behl WOH-moh

attractive	**attraente**	aht-trah-EHN-teh	dirty	**sporco**	SPOHR-koh
beautiful	**bellissimo**	behl-LEES-see-moh	elegant	**elegante**	eh-leh-GAHN-teh
cute	**carino**	kah-REE-noh	fashionable	**alla moda**	AHL-lah MOH-dah
handsome	**bello**	BEHL-loh	neat	**pulito**	poo-LEE-toh
pretty	**grazioso**	grah-TSYOH-zoh	poorly dressed	**mal vestito**	mahl vehs-TEE-toh
ugly	**brutto**	BROOT-toh	untidy	**disordinato**	deez-ohr-dee-NAH-toh
unattractive	**poco attraente**	POH-koh aht-trah-EHN-teh	well-dressed	**ben vestito**	behn vehs-TEE-toh
casually dressed	**vestito casual**	vehs-TEE-toh casual			

very tall	tall	quite tall	not very tall	short
molto alto	**alto**	**abbastanza alto**	**non molto alto**	**basso**
MOHL-toh AHL-toh	AHL-toh	ahb-bah-STAHN-tsah AHL-toh	nohn MOHL-toh AHL-toh	BAHS-soh

She is taller than him.	**Lei è più alta di lui.**	lay EH pyoo AHL-tah dee loo-yee
He isn't as tall as her.	**Lui non è così alto come lei.**	LOO-yee nohn EH koh-ZEE AHL-to KOH-meh lay
She is of average height.	**Lei è di altezza media.**	lay EH dee ahl-TEH-tstsah MEH-dyah

thin	slim	plump	fat
magro	**snello**	**paffuto**	**grasso**
MAHG-roh	ZNEHL-loh	pahf-FOO-toh	GRAHS-soh

slender	**snello**	ZNEHL-loh
skinny	**pelle e ossa**	PEHL-leh eh OHS-sah
obese	**obeso**	oh-BEH-zoh
underweight	**sottopeso**	soht-toh-PEH-zoh
overweight	**sovrappeso**	sohv-rah-PPEH-zoh
She is overweight / underweight.	**Lei è in sovrappeso / sottopeso.**	lay EH een sohv-rah-PPEH-zoh / soht-toh-PEH-zoh
to lose weight	**perdere peso**	PEHR-deh-reh PEH-zoh

grey
grigi
GREE-jee

red
rossi
ROHS-see

dark
scuri
SKOO-ree

black
neri
NEH-ree

blond
biondi
BYOHN-dee

light
chiari
KYAH-ree

chestnut
castani
kahs-TAH-nee

brown
marroni
mahr-ROH-nee

straight	curly	wavy	thick	bald
lisci	**ricci**	**ondulati**	**spessi**	**calvo**
LEE-shee	REE-chchee	ohn-doo-LAH-tee	SPEHS-see	KAHL-voh

long	short	shoulder-length	medium-length	
lunghi	**corti**	**alle spalle**	**di lunghezza media**	
LOON-ghee	KOHR-tee	AHL-leh SPAHL-leh	dee loon-GHEH-tstsah MEH-dyah	

a brunette	**la bruna**	lah BROO-nah
a redhead	**la rossa**	lah ROHS-sah
a blonde	**la bionda**	lah BYOHN-dah
a dark-haired woman	**la donna dai capelli scuri**	lah DOHN-nah day kah-PEHL-lee SCOO-ree
He has long dark hair.	**Lui ha lunghi capelli scuri.**	LOO-yee ah LOON-ghee kah-PEHL-lee SCOO-ree
He has curly hair.	**Lui ha i capelli ricci.**	LOO-yee ah ee kah-PEHL-lee REE-chchee
He is bald.	**Lui è calvo.**	LOO-yee eh KAHL-voh

eyebrows
le sopracciglia
leh SOH-prah-CHCHEEL-yah

eyelashes
le ciglia
leh CHEEL-yah

glasses
gli occhiali
lee ohk-KYAH-lee

sunglasses
gli occhiali da sole
lee ohk-KYAH-lee dah SOH-leh

blue	**azzurri**	ah-DZDZOOR-ree	shortsighted	**miope**	MEE-yoh-peh
grey	**grigi**	GREE-jee	blind	**cieco**	CHYEH-koh
green	**verdi**	VEHR-dee	She wears glasses.	**Lei porta gli occhiali.**	lay POHR-tah lee ohk-KYAH-lee
brown	**marroni**	mahr-ROH-nee	She has blue eyes.	**Lei ha gli occhi azzurri.**	lay ah lee OHK-kee ah-DZDZOOR-ree
dark	**scuri**	SKOO-ree	His eyes are dark brown.	**I suoi occhi sono di colore marrone scuro.**	ee swohy OHK-kee SOH-noh dee koh-LOH-reh mahr-ROH-neh SCOO-roh
light	**chiari**	KYAH-ree			

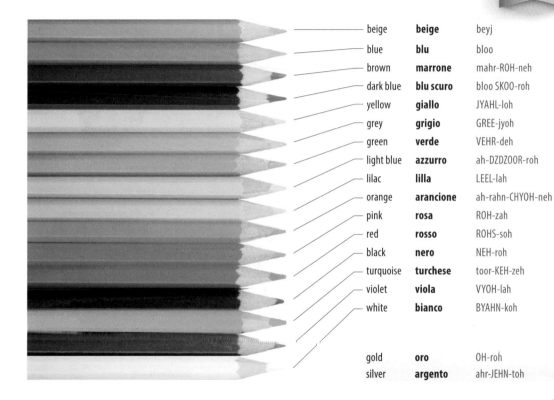

beige	**beige**	beyj
blue	**blu**	bloo
brown	**marrone**	mahr-ROH-neh
dark blue	**blu scuro**	bloo SKOO-roh
yellow	**giallo**	JYAHL-loh
grey	**grigio**	GREE-jyoh
green	**verde**	VEHR-deh
light blue	**azzurro**	ah-DZDZOOR-roh
lilac	**lilla**	LEEL-lah
orange	**arancione**	ah-rahn-CHYOH-neh
pink	**rosa**	ROH-zah
red	**rosso**	ROHS-soh
black	**nero**	NEH-roh
turquoise	**turchese**	toor-KEH-zeh
violet	**viola**	VYOH-lah
white	**bianco**	BYAHN-koh
gold	**oro**	OH-roh
silver	**argento**	ahr-JEHN-toh

positive
positivo
poh-zee-TEE-voh

stubborn
testardo
tehs-TAHR-doh

lucky
fortunato
fohr-too-NAH-toh

dreamer
sognatore
soh-nyah-TOH-reh

visionary
visionario
vee-zyoh-NAH-ryoh

funny
divertente
dee-vehr-TEHN-teh

talkative
loquace
loh-KWAH-cheh

energetic
energico
eh-NEHR-jee-koh

negative
negativo
neh-gah-TEE-voh

creative	**creativo**	kreh-ah-TEE-voh
adventurous	**avventuroso**	ahv-vehn-too-ROH-soh
kind	**gentile**	jehn-TEE-leh
calm	**tranquillo**	trahn-KWEEL-loh
caring	**premuroso**	preh-moo-ROH-zoh
punctual	**puntuale**	poon-too-WAH-leh
crazy	**pazzo**	PAH-tstsoh
frank	**franco**	FRAHN-koh
liar	**bugiardo**	boo-JYAHR-doh
strong	**forte**	FOHR-teh

grandparents
i nonni
ee NOHN-nee

aunt
la zia
lah DZEE-yah

uncle
lo zio
loh DZEE-yoh

parents
i genitori
ee jeh-nee-TOH-ree

sister-in-law
la cognata
lah koh-NYAH-tah

family
la famiglia
lah fah-MEE-lyah

sister
la sorella
lah soh-REHL-lah

brother
il fratello
eel frah-TEHL-loh

cousin (f)
la cugina
lah koo-JEE-nah

cousin
il cugino
eel koo-JEE-noh

nephew
il nipote
eel nee-POH-teh

niece
la nipote
lah nee-POH-teh

myself
me stesso
meh STEHS-soh

wife
la moglie
lah MOH-lyeh

grandchildren	**i nipoti**	ee nee-POH-tee
daughter	**la figlia**	lah FEE-lyah
father	**il padre**	eel PAH-dreh
father-in-law	**il suocero**	eel SWOH-cheh-roh
grandchild	**il nipote / la nipote**	eel nee-POH-teh / lah nee-POH-teh
granddaughter	**la nipota**	la nee POH-teh
grandson	**il nipote**	eel nee-POH-teh
grandfather	**il nonno**	eel NOHN-noh
grandmother	**la nonna**	lah NOHN-nah
great-grandparents	**i bisnonni**	ee bees-NOHN-nee
husband	**il marito**	eel mah-REE-toh
mother	**la madre**	lah MAH-dreh
mother-in-law	**la suocera**	lah SWOH-cheh-rah
son	**il figlio**	eel FEE-lyoh
twin brother	**il fratello gemello**	eel frah-TEHL-loh jeh-MEHL-loh
brother-in-law	**il cognato**	eel koh-NYAH-toh

single child
il figlio unico *m* / la figlia unica *f*
eel FEE-lyoh OO-nee-koh / lah FEE-lyah OO-nee-kah

family with two children
la famiglia con due bambini
lah fah-MEE-lyah kohn DOO-weh bahm-BEE-nee

big family
la famiglia allargata
lah fah-MEE-lyah ahl-lahr-GAH-tah

childless
senza figli
SEHN-tsah FEE-lyee

single father
il padre single
eel PAH-dreh single

single mother
la madre single
lah MAH-dreh single

adoption
l'adozione
lah-doh-TSYO-neh

orphan
l'orfano *m* **/ l'orfana** *f*
LOHR-fah-noh / LOHR-fah-nah

widow
la vedova
lah VEH-doh-vah

stepfather	**il patrigno**	eel pah-TREE-nyoh	to raise	**crescere**	KREH-sheh-reh
stepmother	**la matrigna**	lah mah-TREE-nyah	to be engaged	**essere fidanzato**	EHS-seh-reh fee-dahn-TSAH-to
to be pregnant	**essere incinta**	EHS-seh-reh een-CHEEN-tah	to marry	**sposarsi**	spoh-ZAHR-see
to expect a baby	**essere in attesa di un bambino**	EHS-seh-reh een aht-TEH-zah dee oon bahm-BEE-noh	to be married to	**essere sposato con**	EHS-seh-reh spoh-ZAH-toh kohn
to give birth to	**dare alla luce**	DAH-reh AHL-lah LOO-cheh	divorced	**divorziato**	dee-vohr-TSYAH-toh
born	**nato**	NAH-toh	widowed	**vedovo**	VEH-doh-voh
to baptise	**battezzare**	baht-teh-DZDZAH-reh	widower	**il vedovo**	eel VEH-doh-voh
			to die	**morire**	moh-REE-reh

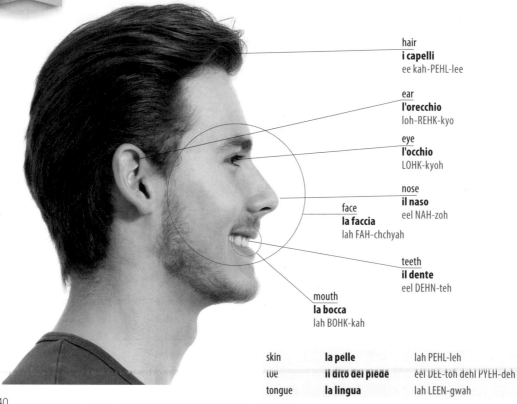

hair
i capelli
ee kah-PEHL-lee

ear
l'orecchio
loh-REHK-kyo

eye
l'occhio
LOHK-kyoh

nose
il naso
eel NAH-zoh

face
la faccia
lah FAH-chchyah

teeth
il dente
eel DEHN-teh

mouth
la bocca
lah BOHK-kah

skin	**la pelle**	lah PEHL-leh
toe	**il dito del piede**	eel DEE-toh dehl PYEH-deh
tongue	**la lingua**	lah LEEN-gwah

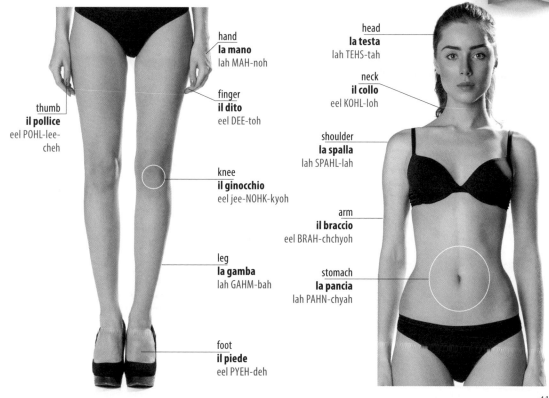

hand
la mano
lah MAH-noh

head
la testa
lah TEHS-tah

neck
il collo
eel KOHL-loh

finger
il dito
eel DEE-toh

thumb
il pollice
eel POHL-lee-cheh

shoulder
la spalla
lah SPAHL-lah

knee
il ginocchio
eel jee-NOHK-kyoh

arm
il braccio
eel BRAH-chchyoh

leg
la gamba
lah GAHM-bah

stomach
la pancia
lah PAHN-chyah

foot
il piede
eel PYEH-deh

angry
arrabbiato
ahr-rahb-BYAH-toh

annoyed
infastdito
een-fahs-tee-DEE-toh

ashamed
vergognoso
vehr-goh-NYOH-zoh

betrayed
tradito
trah-DEE-toh

confused
confuso
kohn-FOO-zoh

confident
fiducioso
fee-doo-CHYOH-zoh

cheated
truffato
troof-FAH-toh

depressed
depresso
deh-PREHS-soh

delighted
contentissimo
kohn-tehn-TEES-see-moh

disappointed
deluso
deh-LOO-zoh

excited
eccitato
eh-chchee-TAH-toh

embarrassed
imbarazzato
eem-bah-rah-TSTSAH-toh

furious
furioso
foo-RYOH-zoh

frightened
spaventato
spah-vehn-TAH-toh

happy
felice
feh-LEE-cheh

horrified
inorridito
een-ohr-ree-DEE-toh

irritated
irritato
eer-ree-TAH-toh

intrigued
incuriosito
een-koo-ryoh-ZEE-toh

jealous
geloso
jeh-LOH-zoh

lazy
pigro
PEE-groh

lucky
fortunato
fohr-too-NAH-toh

relaxed
rilassato
ree-lahs-SAH-toh

sad
triste
TREE-steh

stressed
stressato
strehs-SAH-toh

terrified
terrorizzato
tehr-roh-ree-DZDZAH-toh

upset
sconvolto
skohn-VOHL-toh

unhappy
infelice
een-feh-LEE-cheh

hobby
l'hobby
LOIID-bee

My hobby is …	**Il mio hobby è …**	eel MEE-yoh OHB-bee EH …
Are you interested in …?	**Sei interessato a …?**	say een-teh-rehs-SAH-toh ah …?

baking
la cottura al forno
lah koht-TOO-rah ahl FOHR-noh

coin collecting
il collezionismo di monete
eel kohl-leh-tsyoh-NEEZ-moh dee
moh-NEH-teh

woodworking
la lavorazione del legno
lah lah-voh-rah-TSYOH-neh
dehl LEH-nyoh

stamp collecting
la filatelia
lah fee-lah-teh-LEE-yah

cooking
la cucina
lah koo-CHEE-nah

dance
la danza
lah DAHN-tsah

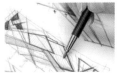

drawing
il disegno
eel dee-ZEH-nyoh

reading
la lettura
lah leht-TOO-rah

jewellery making
la fabbricazione di gioielli
lah fahb-bree-kah-TSYOH-neh
dee joh-YEHL-lee

knitting
la lavorazione a maglia
lah lah-voh-rah-TSYOH-neh ah
MAH-lyah

painting
la pittura
lah peet-TOO-rah

sewing
la cucitura
lah koo-chee-TOO-rah

badminton
il badminton
eel BAHD-meen-tohn

bowling
il bowling
eel BOO-leeng

boxing
il pugilato / la boxe
eel poo-jee-LAH-toh / lah box

chess
gli scacchi
lee SKAHK-kee

cycling
Il ciclismo
eel chee-KLEE-zmoh

darts
le freccette
leh freh-CHCHEHT-teh

diving
l'immersione
leem-mehr-SYOH-neh

fishing
la pesca
lah PEHS-kah

football
il calcio
eel KAHL-chyoh

orienteering
l'orientamento
lohr-yehn-tah-MEHN-toh

gymnastics
la ginnastica
lah jeen-NAHS-tee-kah

handball
la pallamano
lah pahl-lah-MAH-noh

jogging
lo jogging
loh joging

kayaking
il kayak
eel KAH-yahk

martial arts
le arti marziali
leh AHR-tee mahr-TSYAH-lee

mountain biking
la mountain bike
lah mountain bike

paintball
il paintball
eel paintball

photography
la fotografia
lah foh-toh-grah-FEE-yah

rock climbing
l'arrampicata
lahr-rahm-pee-KAH-tah

running
la corsa
lah KOHR-sah

sailing
la vela
lah VEH-lah

surfing
il surf
eel surf

swimming
il nuoto
eel NWOH-toh

table tennis
il tennistavolo
eel tehn-nees-TAH-voh-loh

travel
i viaggi
ee VYAH-djdjee

tennis
il tennis
eel TEHN-nees

yoga
lo yoga
loh YOH-gah

I like to swim.	**Mi piace nuotare.**	mee PYAH-cheh nwoh-TAH-reh
What activities do you like to do?	**Che cosa ti piace fare?**	keh-KOH-zah tee PYAH-cheh FAH-reh?

to get up
alzarsi
ahl-DZAHR-see

to take a shower
fare la doccia
FAH-reh lah DOH-chchyah

to brush your teeth
lavare i denti
lah-VAH-reh ee DEHN-tee

to floss your teeth
pulire i denti con il filo interdentale
poo-LEE-reh ee DEHN-tee kohn eel FEE-loh
een-tehr-dehn-TAH-leh

to shave
farsi la barba
FAHR-see lah BAHR-bah

to brush your hair
pettinarsi
peht-tee-NAHR-see

to put on makeup
truccarsi
trook-KAHR-see

to get dressed
vestirsi
vehs-TEER-see

to get undressed
spogliarsi
spoh-LYAHR-see

to take a bath
fare il bagno
FAH-reh eel BAH-nyoh

to go to bed
andare a letto
ahn-DAH-re ah LEHT-toh

to sleep
dormire
dohr-MEE-reh

Valentine's Day
San Valentino
sahn vah-lehn-TEE-noh

graduation
la laurea
lah LOW-reh-ah

Easter
la Pasqua
lah PAHS-kwah

engagement
il fidanzamento
eel fee-dahn-tsah-MEHN-toh

marriage
il matrimonio
eel mah-tree-MOH-nyoh

bride
la sposa
lah SPOH-zah

Christmas
il Natale
eel nah-TAH-leh

candle
la candela
lah kahn-DEH-lah

present / gift
il regalo
eel reh-GAH-loh

Santa Claus / Father Christmas
il Babbo Natale
eel BAHB-boh nah-TAH-leh

Advent calendar
il calendario dell'Avvento
eel kah-lehn-DAH-ryoh dehl-lahv-VEHN-toh

decoration
la decorazione
lah deh-koh-rah-TSYOH-neh

champagne
lo champagne
loh shahm-PAHN

party
la festa
lah FEH-stah

mistletoe
il vischio
eel VEEH-skyoh

fireworks
i fuochi d'artificio
ee FWOH-kee dahr-tee-FEE-chyoh

birthday
il compleanno
eel kohm-pleh-AHN-noh

ceremony
la cerimonia
lah cheh-ree-MOH-nyah

wedding ring
la fede nuziale
lah FEH-deh noo-TSYAH-leh

decorated eggs
le uova decorate
leh WOH-vah deh-koh-RAH-teh

Easter Bunny
il coniglietto di Pasqua
eel koh-nee-LYEHT-toh dee
PAHS-kwah

New Year	**l'Anno nuovo**	LAHN-noh NWOH-woh
Happy New Year!	**Felice Anno Nuovo!**	feh-LEE-cheh AHN-noh NWOH-voh!
Happy Birthday!	**Buon compleanno!**	bwohn kohm-pleh-AHN-noh!
Congratulations!	**Complimenti!**	kohm-plee-MEHN-tee!

All the best!	**Ti auguro tutto il meglio!**	tee OW-goo-roh TOOT-toh eel MEH-lyoh!
Good luck!	**Buona fortuna!**	BWOH-nah fohr-TOO-nah!
Merry Christmas!	**Buon Natale!**	bwohn nah-TAH-leh!
Happy Easter!	**Buona Pasqua!**	BWOH-nah PAHS-kwah!

Christianity
il cristianesimo
eel kree-styah-NEH-zee-moh

Confucianism
il confucianesimo
eel kohn-foo-chyah-NEH-zee-moh

Jainism
il giainismo
eel jyah-ee-NEEZ-moh

Islam
l'islam
lee-ZLAHM

Buddhism
il buddismo
eel bood-DEEZ-moh

Judaism
il giudaismo
eel jyoo-dah-YEE-zmoh

Hinduism
l'induismo
leen-doo-YEE-zmoh

Taoism
il taoismo
eel tah-oh-YEE-zmoh

Sikhism
il sikhismo
eel see-KEE-zmoh

to confess	**confessarsi**	kohn-fehs-SAHR-see
without religious confession	**senza confessione religiosa**	SEHN-tsah kohn-fehs-SYOH-neh reh-lee-JYOH-zah
to believe in God	**credere in Dio**	KREH-deh-reh een DEE-yoh
to have faith	**essere un credente**	EHS-seh-reh oon kreh-DEHN-teh
to pray	**pregare**	preh-GAH-reh

HOME & HOUSEKEEPING

house
la casa
lah KAH-zah

flat
l'appartamento
lahp-pahr-tah-MEHN-toh

block of flats
il condominio
eel kohn-doh-MEE-nyoh

duplex / two-storey house
la casa bifamiliare / a due piani
lah KAH-zah bee-fah-mee-LYAH-reh /
ah DOO-weh PYAH-nee

detached house
la casa indipendente
lah KAH-zah een-dee-pehn-DEHN-teh

co-ownership
la comproprietà
lah kohm-proh-pryeh-TAH

houseboat
la casa galleggiante
lah KAH-zah gahl-leh-DJDJAHN-teh

caravan
il caravan
eel KAH-rah-vahn

farm
l'azienda agricola
lah-DZYEHN-dah ah-GREE-koh-lah

flatshare
l'appartamento condiviso
lahp-pahr-tah-MEHN-toh
kohn-dee-VEE-zoh

Where do you live?	**Dove vivi?**	DOH-veh VEE-vee?
I live in a flatshare.	**Condivido l'appartamento.**	kohn-dee-VEE-doh lahp-pahr-tah-MEHN-toh
I live with my parents.	**Vivo con i miei genitori.**	VEE-voh kohn ee myay jeh-nee-TOH-ree

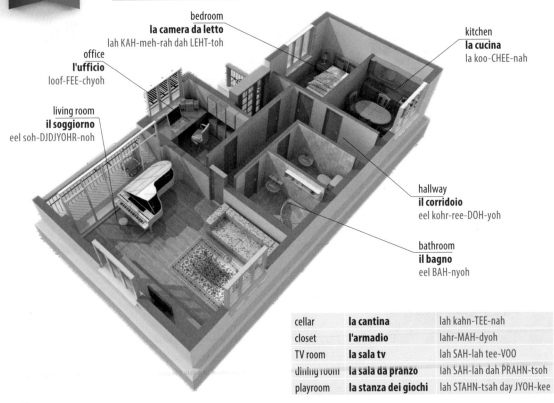

bedroom
la camera da letto
lah KAH-meh-rah dah LEHT-toh

kitchen
la cucina
la koo-CHEE-nah

office
l'ufficio
loof-FEE-chyoh

living room
il soggiorno
eel soh-DJDJYOHR-noh

hallway
il corridoio
eel kohr-ree-DOH-yoh

bathroom
il bagno
eel BAH-nyoh

cellar	**la cantina**	lah kahn-TEE-nah
closet	**l'armadio**	lahr-MAH-dyoh
TV room	**la sala tv**	lah SAH-lah tee-VOO
dining room	**la sala da pranzo**	lah SAH-lah dah PRAHN-tsoh
playroom	**la stanza dei giochi**	lah STAHN-tsah day JYOH-kee

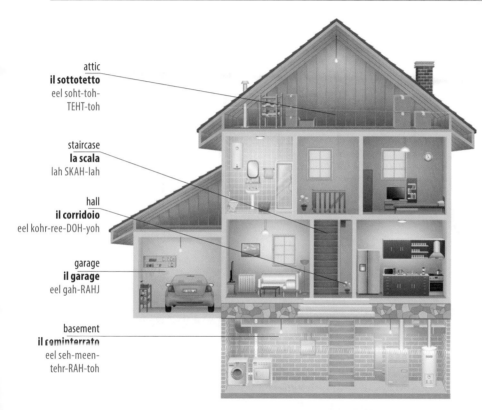

attic
il sottotetto
eel soht-toh-TEHT-toh

staircase
la scala
lah SKAH-lah

hall
il corridoio
eel kohr-ree-DOH-yoh

garage
il garage
eel gah-RAHJ

basement
il seminterrato
eel seh-meen-tehr-RAH-toh

porch
la veranda
lah veh-RAHN-dah

patio
la terrazza
lah tehr-RAH-tstsah

workshop
l'officina
lohf-fee-CHE-nah

window
la finestra
lah fee-NEH-strah

bed
il letto
eel LEHT-toh

lamp
la lampada
lah LAHM-pah-dah

pillow
il cuscino
eel koo-SHEE-noh

chest of drawers
la cassettiera
lah kahs-seht-TYEH-rah

blanket
la coperta
lah koh-PEHR-tah

carpet
il tappeto
eel tahp-PEH-toh

bedsheet
il lenzuolo
eel lehn-TSWOH-loh

bedroom
la camera da letto
lah KAH-meh-rah dah LEHT-toh

bed linen	**la biancheria da letto / le lenzuola**	lah byahn-keh-REE-yah dah LEHT-toh / leh lehn-TSWOH-lah

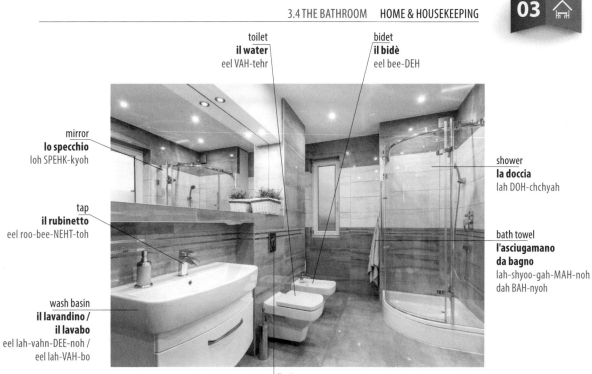

toilet
il water
eel VAH-tehr

bidet
il bidè
eel bee-DEH

mirror
lo specchio
loh SPEHK-kyoh

shower
la doccia
lah DOH-chchyah

tap
il rubinetto
eel roo-bee-NEHT-toh

bath towel
l'asciugamano da bagno
lah-shyoo-gah-MAH-noh dah BAH-nyoh

wash basin
il lavandino / il lavabo
eel lah-vahn-DEE-noh / eel lah-VAH-bo

flush
lo sciaquone
loh shyah-KWOH-neh

bath   **il bagno**   eel BAH-nyoh

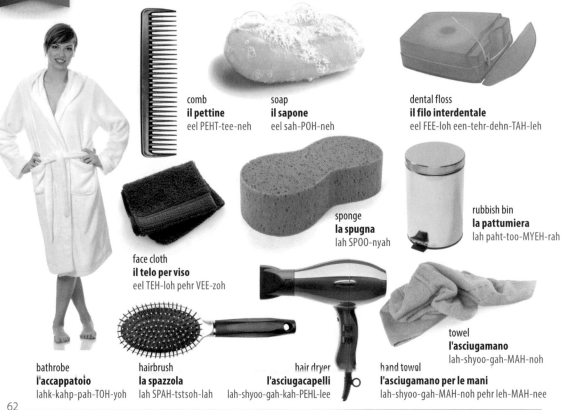

comb
il pettine
eel PEHT-tee-neh

soap
il sapone
eel sah-POH-neh

dental floss
il filo interdentale
eel FEE-loh een-tehr-dehn-TAH-leh

sponge
la spugna
lah SPOO-nyah

rubbish bin
la pattumiera
lah paht-too-MYEH-rah

face cloth
il telo per viso
eel TEH-loh pehr VEE-zoh

towel
l'asciugamano
lah-shyoo-gah-MAH-noh

bathrobe
l'accappatoio
lahk-kahp-pah-TOH-yoh

hairbrush
la spazzola
lah SPAH-tstsoh-lah

hair dryer
l'asciugacapelli
lah-shyoo-gah-kah-PEHL-lee

hand towel
l'asciugamano per le mani
lah-shyoo-gah-MAH-noh pehr leh-MAH-nee

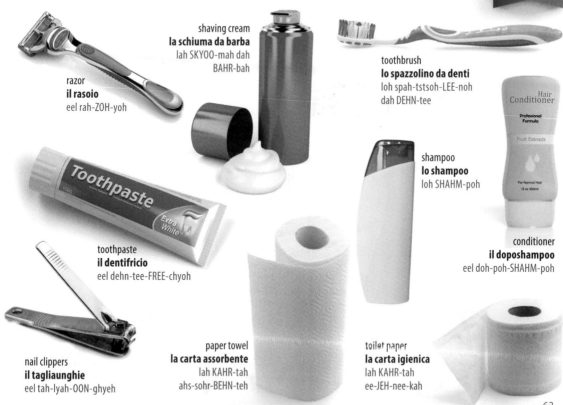

shaving cream
la schiuma da barba
lah SKYOO-mah dah
BAHR-bah

toothbrush
lo spazzolino da denti
loh spah-tstsoh-LEE-noh
dah DEHN-tee

razor
il rasoio
eel rah-ZOH-yoh

shampoo
lo shampoo
loh SHAHM-poh

toothpaste
il dentifricio
eel dehn-tee-FREE-chyoh

conditioner
il doposhampoo
eel doh-poh-SHAHM-poh

nail clippers
il tagliaunghie
eel tah-lyah-OON-ghyeh

paper towel
la carta assorbente
lah KAHR-tah
ahs-sohr-BEHN-teh

toilet paper
la carta igienica
lah KAHR-tah
ee-JEH-nee-kah

microwave
il microonde
eel-me-kroh-OHN-deh

stove
la stufa
lah STOO-fah

coffee machine
la macchina da caffè
lah MAHK-kee-nah
dah kahf-FEH

fridge
il frigo
eel FREE-goh

dishwasher
la lavastoviglie
lah lah-vah-stoh-
VEE-lyeh

freezer
il congelatore
eel kohn-jeh-lah-
TOH-reh

washing machine
la lavatrice
la lah-vah-TREE-cheh

oven
il forno
eel FOHR-noh

kettle
il bollitore
ol bohl-lee-TOH-reh

toaster
Il tostapane
eel toh-stah-PAH-neh

cookery book
il libro di cucina
eel LEE-broh dee koo-CHEE-nah

kitchen roll
il rotolo da cucina
eel ROH-toh-loh dah koo-CHEE-nah

dishcloth
lo strofinaccio
loh stroh-fee-NAH-chchyoh

plug
il tappo
eel TAHP-poh

draining board
lo scolapiatti
loh skoh-lah-PYAHT-tee

tea towel
il canovaccio
eel kah-noh-VAH-chchyoh

shelf
la mensola
lah MEHN-soh-lah

sink
il lavandino
eel lah-vahn-DEE-noh

tablecloth
la tovaglia
lah toh-VAH-lyah

bottle opener
l'apribottiglie
lah-pree-boht-TEE-lyeh

chopping board
il tagliere
eel tah-LYEH-reh

colander
lo scolapasta
loh skoh-lah-PAH-stah

frying pan
la padella
lah pah-DEHL-lah

grater
la grattugia
lah graht-TOO-jyah

juicer
lo spremiagrumi
loh spreh-myah-GROO-mee

corkscrew
il cavatappi
eel kah-vah-TAHP-pee

kitchen scales
la bilancia da cucina
lah bee-LAHN-chyah dah koo-CHEE-nah

mixing bowl
la ciotola
lah CHYOH-toh-lah

sieve
il setaccio
eel seh-TAH-chchyoh

saucepan
la casseruola
lah kahs-sehr-WOH-lah

whisk
la frusta
lah FROO-stah

tin opener
l'apriscatole
lah-pree-SKAH-toh-le

washing-up liquid
il detersivo per piatti
eel deh-tehr-SEE-voh pehr
PYAHT-tee

to do the dishes / to do the washing up	**lavare i piatti**	lah-VAH-reh ee PYAHT-tee
to do the washing	**fare il bucato**	FAH-reh eel buo-KAH-toh
to clear the table	**sparecchiare la tavola**	spah-rehk-KYAH-reh lah TAH-voh-lah
to set the table	**apparecchiare la tavola**	ahp-pah-rehk-KYAH-reh lah TAH-voh-lah

cutlery	**le posate**	leh poh-ZAH-teh
spoon	**il cucchiaio**	eel kook-KYAH-yoh
soup spoon	**il cucchiaio da minestra**	eel kook-KYAH-yoh dah mee-NEH-strah

tablespoon
il cucchiaio da tavola
eel kook-KYAH-yoh dah TAH-voh-lah

fork
la forchetta
lah fohr-KEHT-tah

knife
il coltello
eel kohl-TEHL-loh

teaspoon
il cucchiaino
eel kook-kyah-EE-noh

coffee spoon
il cucchiaino da caffè
eel kook-kyah-EE-noh dah kahf-FEH

plate
il piatto
eel PYAHT-toh

mug
la tazza
lah TAH-tstsah

sugar dispenser
la zuccheriera
lah tsook-keh-RYEH-rah

jug
la caraffa
lah kah-RAHF-fah

saucer
il piattino
eel pyaht-TEE-noh

wine glass
il bicchiere di vino
eel beek-KYEH-reh dee
VEE-noh

teapot
la teiera
lah teh-YEH-rah

cup
la tazza
lah TAH-tstsah

bowl
la ciotola
lah CHYO-toh-lah

jar
il barattolo
eel bah-RAHT-toh-loh

| crockery | **il vasellame** | eel vah-zehl-LAH-meh |
| glass | **il bicchiere** | eel beek-KYEH-reh |

armchair
la poltrona
lah pohl-TROH-nah

sofa
il divano
eel dee-VAH-noh

lampshade
il paralume
eel pah-rah-LOO-meh

lamp
la lampada
lah LAHM-pah-dah

vase
il vaso
eel VAH-zoh

rug
il tappeto
eel tahp-PEH-toh

bookcase
la libreria
lah lee-breh-REE-yah

shelf
la mensola
lah MEHN-soh-lah

plant
la pianta
lah PYAHN-tah

picture
il quadro
eel KWAH-droh

table
il tavolo
eel TAH-voh-loh

chair
la sedia
lah SEH-dyah

I can relax here.	**Posso rilassarmi qui.**	POHS-soh ree-lahs-SAHR-mee kwee
Do you watch TV often?	**Guardi spesso la TV?**	GWAHR-dee SPEHS-soh lah tee-VOO?
What is the size of the living room?	**Qual è la dimensione del soggiorno?**	kwa-LEH lah dee-mehn-SYOH-neh dehl soh-DJDJYOHR-noh?

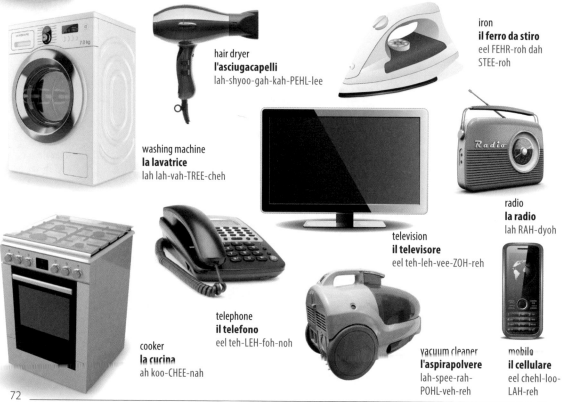

hair dryer
l'asciugacapelli
lah-shyoo-gah-kah-PEHL-lee

iron
il ferro da stiro
eel FEHR-roh dah STEE-roh

washing machine
la lavatrice
lah lah-vah-TREE-cheh

radio
la radio
lah RAH-dyoh

television
il televisore
eel teh-leh-vee-ZOH-reh

telephone
il telefono
eel teh-LEH-foh-noh

cooker
la cucina
ah koo-CHEE-nah

vacuum cleaner
l'aspirapolvere
lah-spee-rah-POHL-veh-reh

mobile
il cellulare
eel chehl-loo-LAH-reh

microwave
il microonde
eel mee-kroh-OHN-deh

kettle
il bollitore
eel bohl-lee-TOH-reh

mixer
il mixer
eel mixer

refrigerator
il frigorifero
eel free-goh-REE-feh-roh

gas stove
il fornello a gas
eel fohr-NEHL-loh-noh ah gahs

coffee grinder
il macinacaffè
eel mah-chee-nah-kahf-FEH

razor
il rasoio
eel rah-ZOH-yoh

juicer
lo spremiagrumi
loh spreh-myah-GROO-mee

sewing machine
la macchina da cucire
la MAHK-kee-nah dah koo-CHEE-reh

blender
il frullatore
eel frool-lah-TOH-reh

to clean up
pulire
poo-LEE-reh

to dust
spolverare
spohl-veh-RAH-reh

to vacuum
passare l'aspirapolvere
pahs-SAH-reh lahs-pee-rah-POHL-veh-reh

to clean the windows
pulire le finestre
poo-LEE-reh leh fee-NEH-streh

to clean the floor
pulire il pavimento
poo-LEE-reh eel pah-vee-MEHN-toh

to do the washing/laundry
lavare i vestiti
lah-VAH-reh ee vehs-TEE-tee

to do the dishes
lavare i piatti
lah-VAH-reh ee PYAHT-tee

to make the bed
fare il letto
FAH-reh eel LEHT-toh

to hang up the laundry
stendere il bucato
STEHN-deh-reh eel boo-KAH-toh

to iron
stirare
stee-RAH-reh

dust cloth
il panno antipolvere
eel PAHN-noh ahn-tee-POHL-veh-reh

bucket
il secchio
eel SEHK-kyoh

feather duster
il piumino
eel pyoo-MEE-noh

mop
il mocio
eel MOH-chyoh

broom
la scopa
lah SCOH-pah

dustpan
la paletta
lah pah-LEHT-tah

clothes line
lo stendibiancheria
loh stehn-dee-byahn-keh-REE-yah

peg
la molletta
lah mohl-LEHT-tah

paper towels
la carta assorbente
lah KAHR-tah ahs-sohr-BEHN-teh

laundry basket
il cesto della biancheria
eel CHEH-stoh DEHL-lah byahn-keh-REE-yah

scrubbing brush
lo spazzolone
loh spah-tstsoh-LOH-neh

window cleaner
il lavavetri
eel lah-vah-VEH-tree

sponge
la spugna
lah SPOO-nyah

detergent
il detergente
eel deh-tehr-JEHN-teh

We have to clean up.	**Dobbiamo fare le pulizie.**	dohb-BYAH-moh FAH-reh leh poo-lee-TSEE-yeh
The flat is already clean.	**L'appartamento è già pulito.**	lahp-pahr-tah-MEHN-toh EH jyah poo-LEE-toh
Who does the cleaning?	**Chi fa le pulizie?**	kee FAH leh poo-lee-TSEE-yeh?

 SCHOOL

white board
la lavagna
lah lah-VAH-nyah

chair
la sedia
lah SEH-dyah

book
il libro
eel LEE-broh

table
la scrivania
lah skree-vah-
NEE-yah

clock
l'orologio
loh-roh-LOH-jyoh

teacher
l'insegnante
leen-seh-NYAHN-teh

student
lo studente
loh stoo-DEHN-teh

tablet
il tablet
eel TAHB-leht

calculator
la calcolatrice
lah kahl-koh-lah-TREE-cheh

to pass	**passare**	pahs-SAH-reh	to go to school	**andare a scuola**	ahn-DAH-reh ah SKWOH-lah
marks	**i voti**	ee VOH-tee	to study	**studiare**	stoo-DYAH-reh
an oral exam	**l'esame orale**	leh-ZAH-meh oh-RAH-leh	to learn	**imparare**	eem-pah-RAH-reh
a written exam	**l'esame scritto**	leh-ZAH-meh SKREET-toh	to do homework	**fare i compiti**	FAH-reh ee COHM-pee-tee
to prepare for an exam	**preparare un esame**	preh-pah-RAH-reh oon eh-ZAH-meh	to know	**sapere**	sah-PEH-reh
to repeat a year	**ripetere un anno**	ree-PEH-teh-reh oon AHN-noh	to take an exam	**dare un esame**	DAH-reh oon eh-ZAH-meh

Languages
le lingue
leh LEEN-gweh

Spanish
lo spagnolo
loh spah-NYOH-loh

German
il tedesco
eel teh-DEH-skoh

English
l'inglese
leen-GLEH-zeh

French
il francese
eel franh-CHEH-zeh

Art
l'arte
LAHR-teh

Geography
la geografia
la jeh-oh-grah-FEE-yah

Music
la musica
lah MOO-zee-kah

History
la storia
lah STOH-ryah

Chemistry
la chimica
lah KEE-mee-kah

Biology
la biologia
lah byoh-loh-JEE-yah

Mathematics
la matematica
lah mah-teh-MAH-tee-kah

Physical education
l'educazione fisica
leh-doo-kah-TSYOH-neh
FEE-zee-kah

scissors
le forbici
leh FOHR-bee-chee

globe
il mappamondo
eel mahp-pah-MOHN-doh

school bag
lo zaino
loh DZAY-noh

pen
la penna
lah PEHN-nah

notebook
il quaderno
eel kwah-DEHR-noh

pencil case
l'astuccio
lah-STOO-chchyoh

ruler
il righello
eel ree-GHEHL-loh

pencil
la matita
lah mah-TEE-tah

pencil sharpener
il temperamatite
eel tehm-peh-rah-mah-TEE-teh

rubber
la gomma
lah GOHM-mah

highlighter
l'evidenziatore
leh-vee-dehn-tsyah-TOH-reh

book
il libro
eel LEE-broh

colouring pen
il pennarello
eel pehn-nah-REHL-loh

stapler
la cucitrice
lah koo-chee-TREE-cheh

WORK

job interview
il colloquio di lavoro
eel kohl-LOH-kwyo dee lah-VOH-roh

candidate
**il candidato m /
la candidata f**
eel kahn-dee-DAH-toh /
lah kahn-dee-DAH-tah

recruiter
il selezionatore
eel seh-leh-tsyoh-
nah-TOH-reh

application letter
**la lettera di
presentazione**
lah LEHT-teh-rah dee
preh-zehn-tah-
TSYOH-neh

CV
il curriculum
eel koor-REE-koo-loom

job advertisement	**l'annuncio di lavoro**	lahn-NOON-chyoh dee lah-VOH-roh
application	**la domanda**	lah doh-MAHN-dah
company	**l'azienda**	lah-DZYEHN-dah
education	**l'istruzione**	lee-stroo-TSYOH-neh
job	**il lavoro**	eel lah-VOH-roh
salary	**lo stipendio**	loh stee-PEHN-dyoh

gross	**lordo**	LOHR-doh
net	**netto**	NEHT-toh
vacancy	**il posto vacante**	eel POH-stoh vah-KAHN-teh
work	**il lavoro**	eel lah-VOH-roh
to fire	**licenziare**	lee-chehn-TSYAH-reh
to hire	**assumere**	ahs-SOO-meh-reh

assessment	**la valutazione**	lah vah-loo-tah-TSYOH-neh
bonus	**il premio**	eel PREH-myoh
employer	**il datore di lavoro**	eel dah-TOH-reh dee lah-VOH-roh
experience	**l'esperienza**	leh-speh-RYEN-tsah
fringe benefits	**le prestazioni accessorie**	leh preh-stah-TSYOH-nee ah-chchehs-SOH-ryeh
maternity leave	**il congedo di maternità**	eel kohn-JEH-doh dee mah-tehr-nee-TAH
notice	**l'avviso**	lahv-VEE-zoh
staff	**il personale**	eel pehr-soh-NAH-leh
human resources officer	**il responsabile delle risorse umane**	eel reh-spohn-SAH-bee-leh DEHL-leh ree-SOHR-seh oo-MAH-neh
promotion	**la promozione**	lah proh-moh-TSYOH-neh
prospects	**le prospettive**	leh proh-speht-TEE-veh
to apply for	**applicare per**	ahp-plee-KAH-reh pehr
to resign	**dimettersi**	dee-MEHT-tehr-see
to retire	**andare in pensione**	ahn-DAH-reh een pehn-SYOH-neh
sick leave	**il congedo per malattia**	eel kohn-JEH-doh pehr mah-laht-TEE-yah
strike	**lo sciopero**	loh SHYOH-peh-roh
trainee	**l'apprendista**	lahp-prehn-DEE-stah
training course	**il corso di formazione**	eel KOHR-soh dee fohr-mah-TSYOH-neh
unemployment benefits	**il sussidio di disoccupazione**	eel soos-SEE-dyoh dee dee-zohk-koo-pah-TSYOH-neh
work place	**il posto di lavoro**	eel POH-stoh dee lah-VOH-roh

employee
l'impiegato *m* /
l'impiegata *f*
leem-pyeh-GAH-toh
leem-pyeh-GAH-tah

actor
l'attore *m* / **l'attrice** *f*
laht-TOH-reh /
laht-TREE-cheh

baker
il fornaio *m* /
la fornaia *f*
eel fohr-NAH-yoh /
lah fohr-NAH-yah

banker
il banchiere *m* /
la banchiera *f*
eel bahn-KYEH-reh /
lah bahn-KYEH-rah

butcher
il macellaio *m* /
la macellaia *f*
eel mah-chehl-LAH-yoh /
lah mah-chehl-LAH-yah

carpenter
il/la falegname *m/f*
eel/lah fah-leh-
NYAH-meh

chef
il cuoco *m* / **la cuoca** *f*
eel KWOH-koh /
lah KWOH-kah

doctor
il medico *m* /
la medica *f*
eel MEH-dee-koh /
lah MEH-dee-kah

farmer
l'agricoltore *m* /
l'agricoltrice *f*
lah-gree-kohl-TOH-reh /
lah-gree-kohl-TREE-cheh

fisherman
il pescatore *m* /
la pescatrice *f*
eel peh-skah-TOH-reh /
lah peh-skah-TREE-cheh

firefighter
il pompiere *m* /
la pompiera *f*
il/la vigile del fuoco *m/f*
eel pohm-PYEH-reh /
lah pohm-PYEH-rah /
eel/lah VEE-jee-leh dehl
FWOH-koh

musician
il musicista *m* /
la musicista *f*
eel moo-zee-
CHEE-stah /
lah moo-zee-
CHEE-stah

lawyer
l'avvocato *m* /
l'avvocata /
l'avvocatessa *f*
lahv-voh-KAH-toh /
lahv-voh-KAH-tah/
lahv-voh-kah-TEHS-sah

nurse
l'infermiere *m* /
l'infermiera *f*
leen-fehr-MYEH-reh / leen-fehr-MYEH-rah

pilot
il/la pilota *m/f*
eel/lah pee-LOH-tah

policeman
il poliziotto *m* /
la poliziotta *f*
eel poh-lee-TSOHT-toh / lah poh-lee-TSYOHT-tah

coach
l'allenatore *m* /
l'allenatrice *f*
lahl-leh-nah-TOH-reh / lahl-leh-nah-TREE-cheh

sailor
il marinaio *m* /
la marinaia *f*
eel mah-ree-NAH-yoh / lah mah-ree-NAH-yah

soldier
il soldato *m* /
la soldata /
soldatessa *f*
eel sohl-DAH-toh / lah sohl-DAH-tah / sohl-dah-TEHS-sah

teacher
l'insegnante *m/f*
leen-seh-NYAH-teh

judge
il giudice *m* /
la giudice *f*
eel JYOO-dee-cheh / lah JYOO-dee-cheh

tailor
il sarto *m* /
la sarta *f*
eel SAHR-toh / lah SAHR-tah

veterinarian
il veterinario *m* /
la veterinaria *f*
eel veh-teh-ree-NAH-ryoh / lah veh-teh-ree-NAH-ryah

waiter
il cameriere *m* /
la cameriera *f*
eel kah-meh-RYEH-reh / lah kah-meh-RYEH-rah

mechanic
il meccanico *m* /
la meccanica *f*
eel mehk-KAH-nee-koh / lah mehk-KAH-nee-kah

engineer	**l'ingegnere** *m/f*	leen-jeh-NYEH-reh
craftsman	**l'artigiano** *m* / **l'artigiana** *f*	Lahr-tee-JYAH-noh / lahr-tee-JYAH-nah
dentist	**il/la dentista** *m/f*	eel/lah dehn-TEE-stah
driver	**l'autista** *m/f*	low-TEE-stah
barber	**il barbiere** *m* / **la parrucchiera** *f*	eel bahr-BYEH-reh / lah pahr-rook-KYEH-rah
beautician	**l'estetista** *m/f*	leh-steh-TEE-stah
broker	**il broker** *m/f*	eel BROH-kehr
accountant	**il/la contabile** *m/f*	eel/lah kohn-TAH-bee-leh
pharmacist	**il/la farmacista** *m/f*	eel/lah fahr-mah-CHEE-stah
writer	**lo scrittore** *m* / **la scrittrice** *f*	loh skreet-TOH-reh / lah skreet-TREE-cheh
politician	**il politico** *m/f*	eel poh-LEE-tee-koh
professor	**il professore** *m* / **la professoressa** *f*	eel proh-fehs-SOH-reh / lah proh-fehs-soh-REHS-sah
salesman	**il venditore** *m* / **la venditrice** *f*	eel vehn-dee-TOH-reh / lah vehn-dee-TREE-cheh
shoemaker	**il calzolaio** *m* / **la calzolaia** *f*	eel kahl-tsoh-LAH-yoh / lah kahl-tsoh-LAH-yah
watchmaker	**l'orologiaio** *m* / **l'orologiaia** *f*	Loh-roh-loh-JYAH-yoh / loh-roh-loh-JYAH-yah
What's your occupation?	**Qual è la tua professione?**	kwah-LEH lah TOO-wah proh-fehs-SYOH-neh?
I work as a secretary.	**Lavoro come segretaria.**	lah-VOH-roh KOH-meh seh-greh-TAH-ryah
I am a teacher.	**Sono un'insegnante.**	SOH-noh oon een-seh-NYAHN-teh

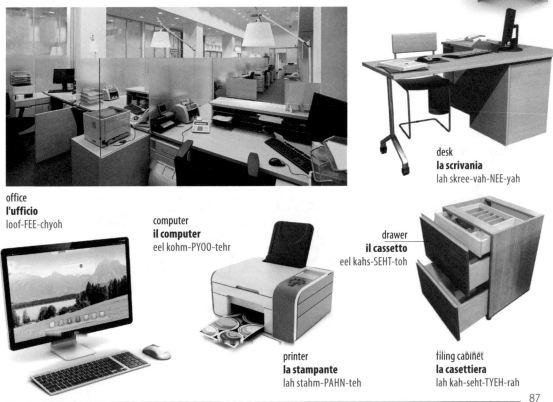

desk
la scrivania
lah skree-vah-NEE-yah

office
l'ufficio
loof-FEE-chyoh

computer
il computer
eel kohm-PYOO-tehr

drawer
il cassetto
eel kahs-SEHT-toh

printer
la stampante
lah stahm-PAHN-teh

filing cabinet
la casettiera
lah kah-seht-TYEH-rah

rubber stamp
il timbro
eel TEEM-broh

telephone
il telefono
eel teh-LEH-foh-noh

ink pad
il tampone per timbri
eel tahm-POH-neh pehr
TEEM-bree

bin
il bidone
eel bee-DOH-neh

swivel chair
la sedia girevole
lah SEH-dyah jee-REH-voh-leh

keyboard
la tastiera
lah tahs-TYEH-rah

clipboard	**la cartella portablocco**	lah kahr-TEHL-lah pohr-tah-BLOHK-koh
file	**il fascicolo**	eel fah-SHEE-koh-loh
to photocopy	**fotocopiare**	foh-toh-koh-PYAH-reh
to print	**stampare**	stahm-PAH-reh

bulldog clip
il fermacarte
eel fehr-mah-KAHR-teh

calculator
la calcolatrice
lah kahl-koh-lah-TREE-cheh

correction tape
il correttore a nastro
eel kohr-reht-TOH-reh ah NAH-stroh

laptop
il portatile
eel pohr-TAH-tee-leh

highlighter
l'evidenziatore
leh-vee-dehn-tsyah-TOH-reh

envelope
la busta
lah BOO-stah

LOREM IPSUM

HEADLINE

holepunch
il perforatore
eel pehr-foh-rah-TOH-reh

elastic bands
gli elastici
lee eh-LAHS-tee-chee

letterhead
la carta intestata
lah KAHR-tah een-tehs-TAH-tah

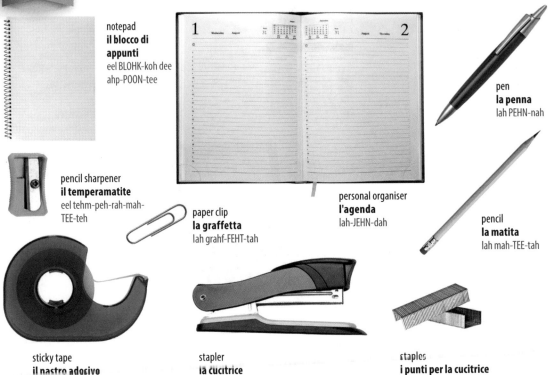

notepad
il blocco di appunti
eel BLOHK-koh dee ahp-POON-tee

pencil sharpener
il temperamatite
eel tehm-peh-rah-mah-TEE-teh

paper clip
la graffetta
lah grahf-FEHT-tah

personal organiser
l'agenda
lah-JEHN-dah

pen
la penna
lah PEHN-nah

pencil
la matita
lah mah-TEE-tah

sticky tape
il nastro adesivo
eel NAH-stroh ah-deh-ZEE-voh

stapler
la cucitrice
lah koo-chee-TREE-cheh

staples
i punti per la cucitrice
ee POON-tee pehr lah koo-chee-TREE-cheh

FOOD AND DRINK

apple juice
il succo di mela
eel SOOK-koh
dee MEH-lah

grapefruit juice
il succo di pompelmo
eel SOOK-koh dee
pohm-PEHL-moh

orange juice
il succo d'arancia
eel SOOK-koh
dah-RAHN-chyah

tomato juice
il succo di pomodoro
eel SOOK-koh dee poh-moh-DOH-roh

coffee
il caffè
eel kahf-FEH

milk
il latte
eel LAHT-teh

tea
il tè
eel teh

with lemon
con limone
kohn lee-MOH-neh

water
l'acqua
LAH-kwah

| with milk | con latte | kohn LAHT-teh | decaffeinated | decaffeinato | deh-kahf-feh-ee-NAH-toh |
| black | nero | NEH-roh | fruit juice | il succo di frutta | eel SOOK-koh dee FROOT-tah |

bacon
la pancetta
lah pahn-CHEHT-tah

banana
la banana
lah bah-NAH-nah

berries
i frutti di bosco
ee FROOT-tee dee BOH-skoh

biscuit
il biscotto
eel bees-KOHT-toh

blueberries
i mirtilli
ee meer-TEEL-lee

bread
il pane
eel PAH-neh

jam
la marmellata
lah mahr-mehl-LAH-tah

butter
il burro
eel BOOR-roh

cereal
i cereali
ee cheh-reh-AH-lee

cheese
il formaggio
eel fohr-MAH-djdjoh

cottage cheese
la ricotta
lah ree-KOHT-tah

doughnut
la ciambella
lah chyahm-BEHL-lah

egg·
l'uovo
LWOH-voh

ham
il prosciutto
eel proh-SHYOOT-toh

honey
il miele
eel MYEH-leh

marmalade
la marmellata
lah mahr-mehl-LAH-tah

omelette
l'omelette
lohm-LEHT

pancake
le crêpes
leh krehps

peanut butter
il burro di arachidi
eel BOOR-roh dee ah-RAH-kee-dee

sandwich
il panino
eel pah-NEE-noh

sausage
la salsiccia
lah sahl-SEE-chchyah

toast
il pane tostato
eel PAH-neh tohs-TAH-toh

waffle
la cialda
lah CHYAL-dah

yoghurt
lo yogurt
loh YOH-goort

breakfast
la colazione
lah koh-lah-TSYOH-neh

brunch
il brunch
eel broonch

porridge
il porridge
eel porridge

scrambled eggs
le uova strapazzate
leh WOH-vah strah-pah-TSTSAH-teh

hard-boiled egg
l'uovo sodo
LWOH-voh SOH-doh

soft-boiled egg
l'uovo alla coque
LWOH-voh AH-lah kohk

What do you eat for breakfast?	**Cosa mangi per colazione?**	KOH-zah MAHN-jee pehr koh-lah-TSYOH-neh?
When do you have breakfast?	**Quando fai la colazione?**	KWAHN-doh fay lah koh-lah-TSYOH-neh?
When does breakfast start?	**Quando inizia la prima colazione?**	KWAHN-doh ee-NEE-tsyah lah PREE-mah koh-lah-TSYOH-neh?
What would you like to drink?	**Che cosa prendi da bere?**	keh KOH-zah PREHN-dee dah BEH-reh?
I would like a white tea.	**Vorrei un tè bianco.**	vohr-RAY oon teh BYAHN-koh

bacon
la pancetta
lah pahn-CHEHT-tah

beef
il manzo
eel MAHN-tsoh

chicken
il pollo
eel POHL-loh

duck
l'anatra
LAH-nah-trah

ham
il prosciutto
eel proh-SHYOOT-toh

kidneys
i rognoni
ee roh-NYOH-nee

lamb
l'agnello
lah-NYEHL-loh

liver
il fegato
eel FEH-gah-toh

mince
la carne macinata
lah KAHR-neh mah-chee-NAH-tah

pâté
il pâté
eel pah-TEH

salami
il salame
eel sah-LAH-meh

meat
la carne
lah KAHR-neh

rabbit
il coniglio
eel koh-NEE-lyoh

pork
la carne di maiale
lah KAHR-neh dee mah-YAH-leh

sausage
la salsiccia
lah sahl-SEE-chchyah

turkey
il tacchino
eel tahk-KEE-noh

veal
il vitello
eel vee-TEHL-loh

fruits
la frutta
lah FROOT-tah

apple
la mela
lah MEH-lah

apricot
l'albicocca
lahl-bee-KOHK-kah

banana
la banana
lah bah-NAH-nah

blackberry
la mora
lah MOH-rah

blackcurrant
il ribes nero
eel REE-behs NEH-roh

blueberry
il mirtillo
eel meer-TEEL-loh

cherry
la ciliegia
lah chee-LYEH-jyah

coconut
il cocco
eel KOHK-koh

fig
il fico
eel FEE-koh

grape
l'uva
LOO-vah

grapefruit
Il pompelmo
eel pohm-PEHL-moh

kiwi fruit
il kiwi
eel KEE-wee

lemon
il limone
eel lee-MOHN-neh

lime
la limetta
lah lee-MEHT-tah

mango
il mango
eel MAHN-goh

melon
il melone
eel meh-LOH-neh

orange
l'arancia
lah-RAHN-chyah

peach
la pesca
lah PEH-skah

pear
la pera
lah PEH-rah

lychee
il litchi
eel LEE-chee

clementine
la clementina
lah kleh-mehn-TEE-nah

papaya
la papaya / la papaia
lah pah-PAH-yah

pineapple
l'ananas
LAH-nah-nahs

watermelon
il cocomero
eel koh-KOH-meh-roh

kumquat
il mandarino cinese
eel mahn-dah-REE-noh
chee-NEH-zeh

raspberry
il lampone
eel lahm-POH-neh

plum
la prugna
lah PROO-nyah

rhubarb
il rabarbaro
eel rah-BAHR-bah-roh

nectarine
la nettarina
lah neht-tah-REE-nah

persimmon
il cachi
eel KAH-kee

redcurrant
il ribes rosso
eel REE-behs ROHS-soh

pomegranate
il melograno
eel meh-loh-GRAH-noh

strawberry
la fragola
lah FRAH-goh-lah

passion fruit
il frutto della passione
eel FROOT-toh DEHL-lah pahs-
SYOH-neh

vegetables
le verdure
leh vehr-DOO-reh

artichoke
il carciofo
eel kahr-CHYOH-foh

asparagus
l'asparago
lah-SPAH-rah-goh

avocado
l'avocado
lah-voh-KAH-doh

beansprouts
i germogli di fagiolo
ee jehr-MOH-lee dee fah-JYOH-loh

beetroot
la barbabietola
lah bahr-bah-BYEH-toh-lah

broccoli
i broccoli
ee BROHK-koh-lee

Brussels sprouts
i cavolini di Bruxelles
ee kah-voh-LEE-nee dee broo-KSEHL

cabbage
il cavolo
eel KAH-voh-loh

aubergine
la melanzana
lah meh-lahn-DZAH-nah

carrot
la carota
lah kah-ROH-tah

101

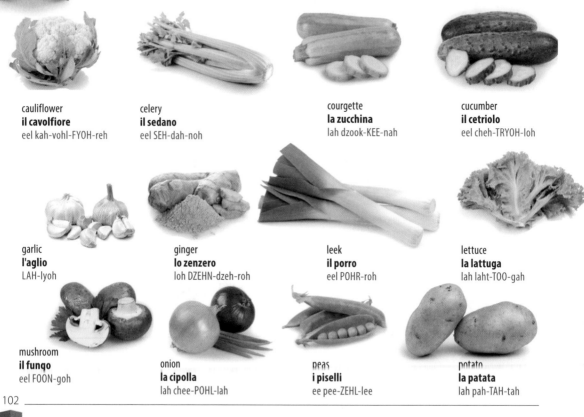

cauliflower
il cavolfiore
eel kah-vohl-FYOH-reh

celery
il sedano
eel SEH-dah-noh

courgette
la zucchina
lah dzook-KEE-nah

cucumber
il cetriolo
eel cheh-TRYOH-loh

garlic
l'aglio
LAH-lyoh

ginger
lo zenzero
loh DZEHN-dzeh-roh

leek
il porro
eel POHR-roh

lettuce
la lattuga
lah laht-TOO-gah

mushroom
il funqo
eel FOON-goh

onion
la cipolla
lah chee-POHL-lah

peas
i piselli
ee pee-ZEHL-lee

potato
la patata
lah pah-TAH-tah

pumpkin
la zucca
lah DZOOK-kah

spinach
gli spinaci
lee spee-NAH-chee

radish
il ravanello
eel rah-vah-NEHL-loh

sweetcorn
il mais
eel mahys

tomato
il pomodoro
eel poh-moh-DOH-roh

spring onion
lo scalogno
loh skah-LOH-nyoh

red pepper
il peperone rosso
eel peh-peh-ROH-neh ROHS-soh

green beans
i fagiolini
ee fah-jyoh-LEE-nee

chicory
l'indivia
leen-DEE-vyah

turnip
la rapa
lah RAH-pah

cuttlefish
la seppia
lah SEHP-pyah

haddock
l'eglefino
leh-gleh-FEE-noh

lemon sole
la sogliola limanda
lah SOH-lyoh-lah lee-MAHN-dah

halibut
l'halibut
LAH-lee-boot

mackerel
lo sgombro
loh ZGOHM-broh

monkfish
la coda di rospo
lah KOH-dah dee ROH-spoh

mussels
le cozze
leh KOH-tstseh

sardine
la sardina
lah sahr-DEE-nah

sea bass
la spigola
lah SPEE-goh-lah

sea bream
l'orata
loh-RAH-tah

swordfish
il pesce spada
eel PEH-sheh SPAH-dah

trout
la trota
lah TROH-tah

crab
il granchio
eel GRAHN-kyoh

crayfish
il gambero
eel GAHM-beh-roh

lobster
l'astice
LAHS-tee-cheh

tuna
il tonno
eel TOHN-noh

octopus
il polpo
eel POHL-poh

oyster
l'ostrica
LOH-stree-kah

prawn / shrimp
il gamberetto
eel gahm-beh-REHT-toh

scallop
il pettine di mare
eel PEHT-tee-neh dee MAH-reh

salmon
il salmone
eel sahl-MOH-neh

squid
il calamaro
eel kah-lah-MAH-roh

fish	**il pesce**	eel PEH-sheh
cleaned	**pulito**	poo-LEE-toh
fresh	**fresco**	FREH-skoh
frozen	**congelato**	kohn-jeh-LAH-toh
salted	**salato**	sah-LAH-toh
skinned	**spellato**	spehl-LAH-toh
smoked	**affumicato**	ahf-foo-mee-KAH-toh

cheese
il formaggio
eel fohr-MAH-djdjoh

cream
la panna
lah PAHN-nah

egg
l'uovo
LWOH-voh

milk
il latte
eel LAHT-teh

cottage cheese
i fiocchi di latte
ee FYOHK-kee dee LAHT-teh

blue cheese
il formaggio blu
eel fohr-MAH-djdjoh bloo

butter
il burro
eel BOOR-roh

goat's cheese	il formaggio di capra	eel fohr-MAH-djdjoh dee KAH-prah	semi-skimmed milk	il latte parzialmente scremato	eel LAHT-teh pahr-tsyahl-MEHN-teh skreh-MAH-toh
crème fraîche	la crème fraîche	lah krehm frehsh	skimmed milk	il latte scremato	eel LAHT-teh skreh-MAH-toh
margarine	la margarina	lah mahr-gah-REE-nah	sour cream	la panna acida	lah PAHN-nah AH-chee-dah
full-fat milk	il latte intero	eel LAHT-teh een-TEH-roh	yoghurt	lo yogurt	loh YOH-goort

baguette
la baguette
lah bah-GEHT

bread rolls
i panini
ee pah-NEE-nee

brown bread
il pane integrale
eel PAH-neh een-teh-GRAH-leh

cake
la torta
lah TOHR-tah

loaf
la pagnotta
lah pah-NYOHT-tah

white bread
il pane bianco
eel PAH-neh BYAHN-koh

garlic bread	il pane all'aglio	eel PAH-neh ahl-LAH-lyoh	quiche	la quiche	lah keesh
pastry	la pasticceria	lah pah-stee-chcheh-REE-yah	sliced loaf	il pane a fette	eel PAH-neh ah FEHT-teh
pitta bread	il pane pita	eel PAH-neh PEE-tah	sponge cake	il pan di Spagna	eel pahn dee SPAH-nyah

ketchup	mayonnaise	mustard	vinegar	salt	pepper
il ketchup	**la maionese**	**la senape**	**l'aceto**	**il sale**	**il pepe**
eel KEH-chahp	lah mah-yoh-NEH-zeh	lah SEH-nah-peh	lah-CHEH-toh	eel SAH-leh	eel PEH-peh

basil	**il basilico**	eel bah-ZEE-lee-koh	paprika	**la paprica**	lah PAH-pree-kah
chilli powder	**la polvere di peperoncino**	lah POHL-veh-reh dee peh-peh-rohn-CHEE-noh	parsley	**il prezzemolo**	eel preh-TSTSEH-moh-loh
chives	**l'erba cipollina**	LEHR-bah chee-pohl-LEE-nah	rosemary	**il rosmarino**	eel rohs-mah-REE-noh
cinnamon	**la cannella**	lah kahn-NEHL-lah	saffron	**lo zafferano**	loh dzahf-feh-RAH-noh
coriander	**il coriandolo**	eel koh-RYAHN-doh-loh	sage	**la salvia**	lah SAHL-vyah
cumin	**il cumino**	eel koo-MEE-noh	salad dressing	**il condimento per insalata**	eel kohn-dee-MEHN-toh pehr een-sah-LAH-tah
curry	**il curry**	eel KEHR-ree	spices	**le spezie**	leh SPEH-tsyeh
dill	**l'aneto**	lah-NEH-toh	thyme	**il timo**	eel TEE-moh
nutmeg	**la noce moscata**	la NOH-cheh moh-SKAH-tah	vinaigrette	**la vinaigrette**	lah vee-neh-GREHT

bag
la borsa
lah BOHR-sah

bar
la barretta
lah bahr-REHT-tah

carton
la scatola di cartone
lah SKAH-toh-lah dee kahr-TOH-neh

bottle
la bottiglia
lah boht-TEE-lyah

jar
il barattolo
eel bah-RAHT-toh-loh

box
la scatola
lah SKAH-toh-lah

pack
il pacco
eel PAHK-koh

packet
il pacchetto
eel pahk-KEHT-toh

punnet
il cestino
eel chehs-TEE-noh

a bag of potatoes	**un sacco di patate**	oon SAHK-koh dee pah-TAH-teh
a bar of chocolate	**una tavoletta di cioccolato**	OO-nah tah-voh-LEHT-tah dee chyohk-koh-LAH-toh
two bottles of mineral water	**due bottiglie di acqua minerale**	DOO-we boht TEE lych dee AIIK wah mee nah RAH-leh
a carton of milk	**una confezione di latte**	OO-nah kohn-feh-TSYOH-neh dee LAHT-teh
a jar of jam	**un barattolo di marmellata**	oon bah-RAHT-toh-loh dee mahr-mehl-LAH-tah

biscuit
il biscotto
eel bee-SKOHT-toh

chocolate bar
la tavoletta di cioccolato
lah tah-voh-LEHT-tah dee chyohk-koh-LAH-toh

chocolate cake
la torta al cioccolato
lah TOHR-tah ahl chyohk-koh-LAH-toh

apple pie
la torta di mele
lah TOHR-tah dee MEH-leh

doughnut
la ciambella
lah chyahm-BEHL-lah

fruit cake
la torta di frutta
lah TOHR-tah dee FROOT-tah

fruit salad
la macedonia
lah mah-cheh-DOH-nyah

cheesecake
la torta di formaggio
lah TOHR-tah dee fohr-MAH-djdjyoh

gingerbread
il pan di zenzero
eel pahn dee DZEHN-dzeh-roh

ice cream
il gelato
eel jeh-LAH-toh

muffin
il muffin
eel MOOF-feen

chocolate mousse
la mousse al cioccolato
lah MOOS ahl chyohk-koh-LAH-toh

milkshake
il frullato
eel frool-LAH-toh

marshmallow
il marshmallow
eel marsh-MAHL-loh

macaroon
l'amaretto
lah-mah-REHT-toh

waffle
la cialda
lah CHYAL-dah

pancakes
le crêpes
leh krehps

strudel
lo strudel
loh STROO-dehl

pudding
il budino
eel boo-DEE-noh

honey
il miele
eel MYEH-leh

cake	**la torta**	lah TOHR-tah
coconut cake	**la torta al cocco**	lah TOHR-tah ahl KOHK-koh
dessert	**il dessert**	eel deh-SEHRT
frozen yoghurt	**lo yogurt gelato**	loh YOH-goort jeh-LAH-toh
rice pudding	**il budino di riso**	eel boo-DEE-noh dee REE-zoh
I like to eat sweets.	**Mi piace mangiare dolci.**	mee PYAH-cheh mahn-JAH-reh DOHL-chee
I cannot eat anything sweet.	**Non posso mangiare dolci.**	nohn POHS-soh mahn-JAH-reh DOHL-chee

cheeseburger
il cheeseburger
eel cheez-BOOR-gher

hot dog
l'hot dog
loht dohg

fish sandwich
il panino di pesce
eel pah-NEE-noh dee PEH-sheh

fried chicken
il pollo arrosto
eel POHL-loh ahr-ROH-stoh

French fries
le patatine fritte
leh pah-tah-TEE-neh FREET-teh

nachos
i nachos
ee NAH-chohs

taco
il taco
eel TAH-koh

burrito
il burrito
eel boor-REE-toh

pizza
la pizza
lah PEE-tstsah

hamburger
l'hamburger
lahm-BOOR-gher

chicken sandwich
il panino di pollo
eel pah-NEE-noh dee POHL-loh

fish and chips
pesce e patatine
PEH-sheh eh pah-tah-TEE-neh

to peel	**sbucciare**	zboo-CHCHYAH-reh
to grate	**grattuggiare**	graht-too-DJDJYAH-reh
to chop	**tritare**	tree-TAH-reh
to crush	**schiacciare**	skyah-CHCHYAH-reh
to beat	**battere**	BAHT-teh-reh
to grease	**ungere**	OON-jeh-reh
to break	**rompere**	ROHM-peh-reh
to stir	**mescolare**	mehs-koh-LAH-reh
to knead	**impastare**	eem-pahs-TAH-reh
to steam	**cuocere al vapore**	KWOH-cheh-reh ahl vah-POH-reh
to weigh	**pesare**	peh-ZAH-reh
to add	**aggiungere**	ah-DJDJYOON-jeh-reh
to bake	**cuocere al forno**	KWOH-cheh-reh ahl FOHR-noh
to stir-fry	**saltare in padella**	sahl-TAH-reh een pah-DEHL-lah
to grill	**grigliare**	gree-LYAH-reh
to roast	**arrostire**	ahr-rohs-TEE-reh
to barbecue	**cuocere ai ferri**	KWOH-cheh-reh ahi FEHR-ree
to fry	**friggere**	FREE-djdjeh-reh

to wash
lavare
lah-VAH-reh

to cut
tagliare
tah-LYAH-reh

to mix
mischiare
mees-KYAH-reh

to boil
bollire
bohl-LEE-reh

bar
il bar
eel bahr

buffet
il buffet
eel boof-FEH

bill
il conto
eel KOHN-toh

bistro
il bistrò
eel bees-TROH

café
il caffè
eel kahf-FEH

dessert
il dessert
eel deh-SEHRT

menu
il menu
eel meh-NOO

canteen
la mensa
lah MEHN-sah

pizzeria
la pizzeria
lah pee-tstseh-REE-yah

pub
il pub
eel pahb

salad bar
il buffet di insalate
eel boo-FEH dee een-sah-LAH-teh

deli
i prodotti di gastronomia
ee proh-DOHT-tee dee gahs-troh-noh-MEE-yah

115

self-service
self-service
self-service

take-out / take-away
da asporto / da portare via
da ahs-POHR-toh / dah pohr-TAH-reh VEE-yah

waiter
il cameriere
eel kah-meh-RYEH-reh

waitress
la cameriera
lah kah-meh-RYEH-rah

à la carte	**à la carte**	ah lah kahrt
starter	**l'antipasto**	lahn-tee-PAH-stoh
booking	**la prenotazione**	lah preh-noh-tah-TSYOH-neh
complimentary	**in omaggio**	een oh-MAH-djdjoh
dish	**il piatto**	eel PYAHT-toh
main course	**il piatto principale**	eel PYAHT-toh preen-chee-PAH-leh
to order	**ordinare**	ohr-dee-NAH-reh
speciality	**la specialità**	lah speh-chyah-lee-TAH
aperitif	**l'aperitivo**	lah-peh-ree-TEE-voh

What do you want to order?	**Che cosa prendi?**	keh KOH-zah PREHN-dee?
I would like to see the menu.	**Vorrei il menu.**	vohr-RAY eel meh-NOO
We'll take the set menu.	**Prenderemo il menu fisso.**	phren-deh-REH-moh eel meh-NOO FEES-soh

TRAVEL AND LEISURE

to travel by bus
viaggiare in autobus
vyah-DJDJAH-reh een OW-toh-boos

to travel by plane
viaggiare in aereo
vyah-DJDJAH-reh een
ah-EH-reh-oh

to travel by car
viaggiare in macchina
vyah-DJDJAH-reh een-MAHK-
kee-nah

to travel by bicycle
viaggiare in bicicletta
vyah-DJDJAH-reh een-bee-
chee-KLEHT-tah

to travel by motorcycle
viaggiare in moto
vyah-DJDJAH-reh een-
MOH-toh

travel agency
l'agenzia di viaggio
lah-jehn-TSEE-yah dee
VYAH-djdjyoh

family holiday
la vacanza in famiglia
lah vah-KAHN-tshah een fah-
MEE-lyah

safari
il safari
eel sah-FAH-ree

beach holiday
le vacanze al mare
leh vah-KAHN-tseh ahl MAH-reh

honeymoon
la luna di miele
lah LOO-nah dee MYEH-leh

round-the-world trip
il giro del mondo
eel JEE-roh dehl MOHN-doh

cruise
la crociera
lah kroh-CHYEH-rah

to book
prenotare
preh-noh-TAH-reh

long-haul destination
la destinazione a lungo raggio
lah deh-stee-nah-TSYOH-neh ah
LOON-goh RAH-djdjyoh

guided tour
la visita guidata
lah VEE-zee-tah gwee-DAH-tah

out of season
fuori stagione
FWOH-ree stah-JYOH-neh

picturesque village
il pittoresco villaggio
eel peet-toh-REH-skoh
veel-LAH-djdjoh

landscape
il paesaggio
eel pah-eh-ZAH-djdjyoh

to go sightseeing
andare a visitare
ahn-DAH-reh ah vee-zee-TAH-reh

city break
il viaggio in città
eel VYAH-djdjyoh een
cheet-TAH

holiday brochure	**l'opuscolo**	loh-POOS-koh-loh
holiday destination	**la destinazione turistica**	lah deh-stee-nah-TSYOH-neh too-REE-stee-kah
package tour	**il pacchetto turistico**	eel pahk-KEHT-toh too-REE-stee-koh
places of interest	**i luoghi di interesse**	ee LWOH-ghee dee een-teh-REHS-seh
short break	**la breve pausa**	lah BREH-veh POW-zah
tourist attractions	**le attrazioni turistiche**	leh aht-trah-TSYOH-nee too-REES-tee-keh
tourist trap	**la trappola per turisti**	lah TRAHP-poh-lah pehr too-REE-stee

Afghanistan
l'Afghanistan
lahf-gah-nee-STAHN

Angola
l'Angola
lahn-GOH-lah

Aruba
l'Aruba
lah-ROO-bah

The Bahamas
le Bahamas
leh bah-AH-mas

Belarus
la Bielorussia
lah byeh-loh-ROOS-yah

Albania
l'Albania
lahl-bah-NEE-yah

Antigua and Barbuda
l'Antigua e Barbuda
lahn-TEE-gwah eh bahr-BOO-dah

Australia
l'Australia
low-STRAH-lyah

Bahrain
il Bahrain
eel bah-REHYN

Belgium
il Belgio
eel BEHL-jyoh

Algeria
l'Algeria
lahl-jeh-REE-yah

Argentina
l'Argentina
lahr-jehn-TEE-nah

Austria
l'Austria
LOW-stryah

Bangladesh
il Bangladesh
eel bahn-glah-DESH

Belize
il Belize
eel beh-LEE-zeh

Andorra
l'Andorra
lahn-DOHR-rah

Armenia
l'Armenia
lahr-MEH-nyah

Azerbaijan
l'Azerbaigian
lah-dzehr-bahy-DJAHN

Barbados
il Barbados
eel bahr-BAH-dohs

Benin
il Benin
eel beh-NEEN

Bhutan
il Bhutan
eel boo-TAHN

Brazil
il Brasile
eel brah-ZEE-leh

Burma
la Birmania
lah beer-MAH-nyah

Canada
il Canada
eel KAH-nah-dah

Chile
il Cile
eel CHEE-leh

Bolivia
la Bolivia
lah boh-LEE-vyah

Brunei
il Brunei
eel broo-NEY

Burundi
il Burundi
eel boo-ROON-dee

Cape Verde
il Capo Verde
eel KAH-poh VEHR-deh

China
la Cina
lah CHEE-nah

Bosnia and Herzegovina
la Bosnia-Erzegovina
lah BOH-znyah ehr-tseh-GOH-vee-nah

Bulgaria
la Bulgaria
lah bool-gah-REE-yah

Cambodia
la Cambogia
lah kahm-BOH-jyah

Central African Republic
la Repubblica Centrafricana
lah reh-POOB-blee-kah chehn-trah-free-KAH-nah

Colombia
la Colombia
la koh-LOHM-byah

Botswana
la Botswana
lah boh-TSWAH-nah

Burkina Faso
Il Burkina Faso
eel boor-KEE-nah FAH-zoh

Cameroon
il Camerun
eel KAH-meh-roon

Chad
il Ciad
eel chyad

Comoros
le Comore
leh koh-MOH-reh

Democratic Republic
of the Congo
**la Repubblica
Democratica del Congo**
lah reh-POOB-blee-kah deh-
moh-KRAH-tee-kah dehl
KOHN-goh

Republic of the Congo
la Repubblica del Congo
lah reh-POOB-blee-kah dehl
KOHN-goh

Costa Rica
la Costa Rica
lah KOHS-tah REE-kah

Côte d'Ivoire
la Costa d'Avorio
lah KOHS-tah dah-VOHR-yoh

Croatia
la Croazia
lah kroh-AH-tsyah

Cuba
la Cuba
lah KOO-bah

Curacao
Curaçao
koo-rah-SSAH-oh

Cyprus
il Cipro
eel CHEE-proh

Czechia
la Repubblica Ceca
lah reh-POOB-blee-kah
CHEH-kah

Denmark
la Danimarca
lah dah-nee-MAHR-kah

Djibouti
la Repubblica di Gibuti
lah reh-POOB-blee-kah
dee jee-BOO-tee

Dominica
la Dominica
lah doh-mee-NEE-kah

Dominican Republic
la Repubblica Dominicana
lah reh-POOB-blee-kah doh-
mee-nee-KAH-nah

East Timor
il Timor Est
eel TEE-mohr ehst

Ecuador
l'Ecuador
leh-kwah-DOHR

Egypt
l'Egitto
leh-JEET-toh

El Salvador
El Salvador
ehl sahl-vah-DOHR

Equatorial Guinea
la Guinea Equatoriale
lah gwee-NEH-ah
eh-kwah-toh-RYAH-leh

Eritrea
l'Eritrea
leh-ree-TREH-ah

Estonia
l'Estonia
leh-STOH-nyah

France
la Francia
lah FRAHN-chya

Germany
la Germania
lah jehr-MAH-nyah

Guatemala
la Guatemala
lah gwah-teh-MAH-lah

Haiti
Haiti
ah-YEE-tee

Ethiopia
l'Etiopia
leh-TYOH-pyah

Gabon
il Gabon
eel gah-BOHN

Ghana
la Ghana
lah GAH-nah

Guinea
la Guinea
lah gwee-NEH-ah

Honduras
l'Honduras
lohn-DOO-rahs

Fiji
le Figi
leh FEE-jee

The Gambia
la Gambia
lah GAHM-byah

Greece
la Grecia
lah GREH-chyah

Guinea-Bissau
la Guinea-Bissau
lah gwee-NEH-ah bees-SOW

Hong Kong
l'Hong Kong
lohng kohng

Finland
la Finlandia
lah feen-LAHN-dyah

Georgia
la Georgia
lah jeh-OHR-jyah

Grenada
la Grenada
lah greh-NAH-dah

Guyana
la Guiana
lah goo-YAH-nah

Hungary
l'Ungheria
loon-gheh-REE-yah

Iceland
l'Islanda
leez-LAHN-dah

Iraq
l'Iraq
lee-RAHK

Jamaica
la Giamaica
lah jyah-MAHY-kah

Kenya
la Kenia
lah KEH-nyah

Kosovo
il Kosovo
eel KOH-soh-voh

India
l'India
LEEN-dyah

Ireland
l'Irlanda
leer-LAHN-dah

Japan
il Giappone
eel jyahp-POH-neh

Kiribati
le Kiribati
leh kee-ree-BAH-tee

Kuwait
il Kuwait
eel koo-WEHYT

Indonesia
l'Indonesia
leen-doh-NEH-zyah

Israel
l'Israele
leez-rah-EH-leh

Jordan
la Giordania
lah jyohr-DAH-nyah

North Korea
la Corea del Nord
lah koh-REH-ah dehl NOHRD

Kyrgyzstan
il Kirghizistan
eel keer-gee-dzee-STAHN

Iran
l'Iran
lee-RAHN

Italy
l'Italia
lee-TAHL-yah

Kazakhstan
il Kazakistan
eel kah-dzah-kee-STAHN

South Korea
la Corea del Sud
lah koh-REH-ah dehl SUUD

Laos
il Laos
eel LAH-ohs

Latvia
la Lettonia
lah leht-TOH-nyah

Libya
la Libia
lah LEE-byah

Macau
il Macao
eel mah-KAW

Malaysia
la Malaysia
lah mah-lah-YEE-zyah

Marshall Islands
le Isole Marshall
leh EE-zoh-leh
MAHR-shahl

Lebanon
il Libano
eel LEE-bah-noh

Liechtenstein
il Liechtenstein
eel LEEK-tehn-shtahyn

Macedonia
la Macedonia
lah mah-cheh-DOH-nyah

Maldives
le Maldive
leh mahl-DEE-veh

Mauritania
la Mauritania
lah mow-ree-TAH-
nyah

Lesotho
il Lesotho
eel leh-SOH-toh

Lithuania
la Lituania
lah lee-too-AH-nyah

Madagascar
il Madagascar
eel mah-dah-gah-SKAHR

Mali
il Mali
eel MAH-lee

Mauritius
il Maurizio
eel mow-REE-tsyoh

Liberia
la Liberia
lah lee-BEH-ryah

Luxembourg
il Lussemburgo
eel loos-sehm-BOOR-goh

Malawi
il Malawi
eel mah-LAH-wee

Malta
la Malta
lah MAHL-tah

Mexico
il Messico
eel MEHS-see-koh

Micronesia
la Micronesia
lah mee-kroh-NEH-zyah

Montenegro
il Montenegro
eel mohn-teh-NEH-groh

Nauru
il Nauru
eel nah-OO-roo

Nicaragua
la Nicaragua
lah nee-kah-RAH-gwah

Oman
l'Oman
loh-MAHN

Moldova
la Moldavia
lah mohl-DAH-vyah

Morocco
il Marocco
eel mah-ROHK-koh

Nepal
il Nepal
neh-PAHL

Niger
il Niger
eel NEE-jehr

Pakistan
il Pakistan
eel pah-kee-STAHN

Monaco
il Monaco
eel MOH-nah-koh

Mozambique
il Mozambico
eel moh-zahm-BEE-koh

Netherlands
l'Olanda
loh-LAHN-dah

Nigeria
la Nigeria
lah nee-JEH-ryah

Palau
Palau
pah-LAW

Mongolia
la Mongolia
lah-mohn-GOH-lyah

Namibia
la Namibia
lah nah-MEE-byah

New Zealand
la Nuova Zelanda
lah NWOH-vah dzeh-
LAHN-dah

Norway
la Norvegia
lah nohr-VEH-jyah

Palestinian Territories
i Territori palestinesi
ee tehr-ree-TOH-ree
pah-leh-stee-NEH-zee

Panama
il Panama
eel PAH-nah-mah

Peru
il Perù
eel peh-ROO

Qatar
il Qatar
eel KAH-tahr

Saint Lucia
la Santa Lucia
lah SAHN-tah loo-
CHEE-yah

Senegal
il Senegal
eel SEH-neh-gahl

Papua New Guinea
la Papua Nuova Guinea
lah PAH-pwah NWOH-vah
gwee-NEH-ah

Philippines
le Filippine
leh fee-leep-PEE-neh

Romania
la Romania
lah roh-mah-NEE-yah

Samoa
la Samoa
lah sah-MOH-ah

Serbia
la Serbia
lah SEHR-byah

Paraguay
il Paraguay
eel pah-rah-GWAHY

Poland
la Polonia
lah poh-LOH-nyah

Russia
la Russia
lah ROOS-syah

San Marino
San Marino
sahn mah-REE-noh

Seychelles
le Seychelles
leh say-SHEHL

Portugal
Il Portogallo
eel pohr-toh-GAHL-loh

Rwanda
la Ruanda
lah roo-AHN-dah

Saudi Arabia
l'Arabia Saudita
lah-RAH-byah
sow-DEE-tah

Sierra Leone
la Sierra Leone
lah SYEHR-rah
leh-OH-neh

Singapore
la Singapore
lah seen-gah-POH-reh

Solomon Islands
le Isole Salomone
leh EE-zoh-leh sah-loh-MOH-neh

Sri Lanka
la Sri Lanka
lah sree LAHN-kah

Swaziland
lo Swaziland
loh SWAH-zee-lahnd

Taiwan
il Taiwan
eel tahy-WAHN

Sint Maarten
Sint Maarten
seent MAHR-tehn

Somalia
la Somalia
lah soh-MAH-lyah

Sudan
il Sudan
eel soo-DAHN

Sweden
la Svezia
lah ZVEH-tsyah

Tajikistan
il Tagikistan
eel tah-jee-kee-STAHN

Slovakia
la Slovacchia
lah zloh-VAHK-kyah

South Africa
la Sudafrica
lah sood-AH-free-kah

South Sudan
il Sudan del Sud
eel soo-DAHN dehl SOOD

Switzerland
la Svizzera
lah ZVEE-tstseh-rah

Tanzania
la Tanzania
lah tahn-DZAH-nyah

Slovenia
la Slovenia
lah zloh-VEH-nyah

Spain
la Spagna
lah SPAH-nyah

Suriname
il Suriname
eel soo-ree-NAH-meh

Syria
la Siria
lah SEE-ryah

Thailand
la Thailandia
lah thay-LAHN-dyah

Togo
il Togo
eel TOH-goh

Turkey
la Turchia
lah toor-KEE-yah

Ukraine
l'Ucraina
loo-krah-EE-nah

Uruguay
l'Uruguay
loo-roo-GWAY

Vietnam
il Vietnam
eel vyeht-NAHM

Tonga
le Tonga
leh TOHN-gah

Turkmenistan
il Turkmenistan
eel toork-meh-nee-STAHN

United Arab Emirates
gli Emirati Arabi Uniti
lee eh-mee-RAH-tee
AH-rah-bee oo-NEE-tee

Uzbekistan
l'Uzbekistan
loo-dzbeh-kee-STAHN

Yemen
lo Yemen
loh JEH-mehn

Trinidad and Tobago
Trinidad e Tobago
tree-nee-DAHD eh
toh-BAH-goh

Tuvalu
Tuvalu
too-VAH-loo

United Kingdom
il Regno Unito
eel REH-nyoh oo-NEE-toh

Vanuatu
Vanuatu
vah-noo-AH-too

Zambia
lo Zambia
loh DZAHM-byah

Tunisia
la Tunisia
lah too-nee-ZEE-yah

Uganda
l'Uganda
loo-GAHN-dah

United States of America
gli Stati Uniti d'America
lee STAH-tee oo-NEE-tee
dah-MEH-ree-kah

Venezuela
la Venezuela
lah veh-neh-ZWEH-lah

Zimbabwe
lo Zimbabwe
loh dzeem-BAH-
bweh

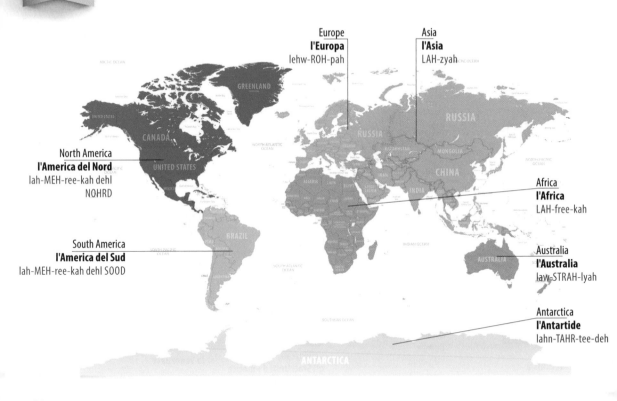

Europe
l'Europa
lehw-ROH-pah

Asia
l'Asia
LAH-zyah

North America
l'America del Nord
lah-MEH-ree-kah dehl
NOHRD

Africa
l'Africa
LAH-free-kah

South America
l'America del Sud
lah-MEH-ree-kah dehl SOOD

Australia
l'Australia
law-STRAH-lyah

Antarctica
l'Antartide
lahn-TAHR-tee-deh

bus stop
la fermata dell'autobus
lah fehr-MAH-tah dehl-OW-
toh-boos

platform
il binario
eel bee-NAH-ryoh

(aero)plane
l'aereo
lah-EH-reh-oh

moped / scooter
il motorino / lo scooter
eel moh-toh-REE-noh /
loh SKOO-tehr

(bi)cycle
la bicicletta / la bici
lah bee-chee-KLEHT-tah /
lah BEE-chee

boat
la barca
lah BAHR-kah

bus
l'autobus / il pullman
LOW-toh-boos / eel POOL-mahn

ship
la nave
lah NAH-veh

car
la macchina
lah MAHK-kee-nah

helicopter
l'elicottero
leh-lee-KOHT-teh-roh

lorry
il camion
eel KAH-myohn

tanker
la petroliera
lah peh-troh-LYEH-rah

kids' scooter
il monopattino
eel moh-noh-PAHT-tee-noh

(motor)bike
la moto(cicletta)
lah MOH-toh / lah moh-toh-
chee-KLEHT-tah

train
il treno
eel TREH-noh

taxi
il tassì
eel tahs-SEE

ferry
il traghetto
eel trah-GHEHT-toh

submarine
il sottomarino
eel soht-toh-mah-REE-noh

yacht
lo yacht / la barca a vela
loh yoht / lah BAHR-kah ah
VEH-lah

tram
il tram
eel trahm

by air	**per via aerea**	pehr VEE-yah ah-EH-reh-ah	in the port	**al porto**	ahl POHR-toh
on the motorway	**sull'autostrada**	sool-low-toh-STRAH-dah	by rail	**in treno**	een TREH-noh
on the road	**sulla strada**	SOOL-lah STRAH-dah	by tube / underground	**in metropolitana**	een meh-troh-poh-lee-TAH-nah
by sea	**via mare**	VEE-yah MAH-reh	on foot	**a piedi**	ah PYEH-dee

airport
l'aeroporto
lah-eh-roh-POHR-toh

arrivals
gli arrivi
lee ahr-REE-vee

departures
le partenze
leh pahr-TEHN-tseh

luggage
il bagaglio
eel bah-GAH-lyoh

carry-on luggage
il bagaglio a mano
eel bah-GAH-lyoh ah MAH-noh

oversized baggage
il bagaglio fuori misura
eel bah-GAH-lyoh FWOH-ree mee-ZOO-rah

check-in desk
il banco del check-in
eel BAHN-koh dehl chehk-EEN

customs
la dogana
lah doh-GAH-nah

baggage reclaim
il ritiro bagagli
eel ree-TEE-roh bah-GAH-lyee

boarding pass
la carta d'imbarco
lah CAHR-tah deem-BAHR-koh

flight ticket
il biglietto aereo
eel bee-LYEHT-toh ah-EH-reh-oh

economy class
la classe turistica
lah KLAHS-seh too-REES-tee-kah

business class
la classe business
lah KLAHS-seh BEEZ-nehs

arrivals lounge
la sala arrivi
lah-SAH-lah ahr-REE-vee

delayed
in ritardo
een ree-TAHR-doh

to board a plane
imbarcarsi su un aereo
eem-bahr-KAHR-see soo oon
ah-EH-reh-oh

gate
la uscita d'imbarco
loo-SHEE-tah deem-BAHR-koh

passport
il passaporto
eel pahs-sah-POHR-toh

passport control
il controllo passaporti
eel kohn-TROHL-loh
pahs-sah-POHR-tee

security check
il controllo di sicurezza
eel kohn-TROHL-loh dee see-
koo-REH-tstsah

airline	**la compagnia aerea**	lah kohm-pah-NEE-yah ah-EH-reh-ah		on time	**puntualmente**	poon-too-ahl-MEHN-teh
boarding time	**l'orario d'imbarco**	loh-RAHR-yoh deem-BAHR-koh		return ticket	**il biglietto di andata e ritorno**	eel bee-LYEHT-toh dee ahn-DAH-tah eh ree-TOHR-noh
charter flight	**il volo charter**	eel VOH-loh CHAHR-tehr		The flight has been delayed.	**Il volo ha subito un ritardo.**	eel VOH-loh ah soo-BEE-toh oon ree-TAHR-doh.
long-haul flight	**il volo a lungo raggio**	eel VOH-loh ah LOON-goh RAH-djdjyoh		to book a ticket to	**prenotare un biglietto per**	preh-noh-TAH-reh oon bee-LYEHT-toh pehr
one-way ticket	**il biglietto di sola andata**	eel bee-LYEHT-toh dee SOH-lah ahn-DAH-tah				

railway station
la stazione ferroviaria
lah stah-TSYOH-neh
fehr-roh-VYAH-ryah

train
il treno
eel TREH-noh

platform
il binario
eel bee-NAH-ryoh

express train	il treno espresso	eel TREH-noh ehs-PREHS-soh
to get on the train	salire sul treno	sah-LEE-reh sool TREH-noh
to get off the train	scendere dal treno	SHEHN-deh-reh dahl TREH-noh
to miss a train	perdere il treno	PEHR-deh-reh eel TREH-noh

train driver
il macchinista
eel mahk-kee-NEE-stah

travelcard
l'abbonamento
lahb-boh-nah-MEHN-toh

carriage
la carrozza
lah kahr-ROH-tstsah

seat
il sedile / il posto
eel seh-DEE-leh / eel POH-stoh

train journey
il viaggio in treno
eel VYAH-djdjyoh een TREH-noh

station
la stazione
lah stah-TSYOH-neh

restaurant car
la carrozza ristorante
lah kahr-ROH-tstsah rees-toh-RAHN-teh

sleeper train
il treno notturno
eel TREH-noh noht-TOOR-noh

toilet
il bagno
eel BAH-nyoh

bus
l'autobus
LOW-toh-boos

bus driver
l'autista dell'autobus
low-TEE-stah dehl-LOW-toh-boos

bus stop
la fermata dell'autobus
lah fehr-MAH-tah
dehl-LOW-toh-boos

validator
l'obliteratrice
loh-blee-teh-rah-TREE-cheh

double-decker bus
l'autobus a due piani
LOW-toh-boos ah DOO-weh
PYAH-nee

bus journey
il viaggio in autobus
eel VYAH-djdjyoh een
OW-toh-boos

coach station
la stazione degli autobus
lah stah-TSYOH-neh DEHL-lee
OW-toh-boos

request stop
la fermata a richiesta
lah fehr-MAH-tah ah ree-
KYEH-stah

bus fare	**il prezzo del biglietto dell'autobus**	eel PREH-tstsoh dehl bee-LYEHT-toh dehl-LOW-toh-boos
the next stop	**la prossima fermata**	lah PROHS-see-mah fehr-MAH-tah
night bus	**l'autobus notturno**	LOW-toh-boos noht-TOOR-noh
to get on the bus	**salire sull'autobus**	sah-LEE-reh sool-LOW-toh-boos
to get off the bus	**scendere dall'autobus**	SHEHN-deh-reh dahl-LOW-toh-boos
to miss a bus	**perdere l'autobus**	PEHR-deh-reh LOW-toh-boos

hotel
l'albergo
lahl-BEHR-goh

campsite
il campeggio
eel kahm-PEH-djdjyoh

holiday resort
la località di villeggiatura
lah loh-kah-lee-TAH dee veel-
leh-djdjyah-TOO-rah

youth hostel
l'ostello della gioventù
lohs-TEHL-loh DEHL-lah jyoh-
vehn-TOO

accommodation	**l'alloggio**	lahl-LOH-djdjyoh
all-inclusive	**tutto compreso**	TOOT-toh kohm-PREH-zoh
half-board	**la mezza pensione**	lah MEH-dzdzah pehn-SYOH-neh
full-board	**la pensione completa**	lah pehn-SYOH-neh kohm-PLEH-tah
self-catering	**con uso cucina**	kohn OO-zoh koo-CHEE-nah
I'm looking for a place to stay.	**Sto cercando un posto dove alloggiare.**	stoh chehr-KAHN-doh oon POH-stoh DOH-veh ahl-loh-DJDJAYH-reh
Can you recommend a hotel?	**Puoi raccomandarmi qualche albergo?**	pwoy rahk-koh-mahn-DAHR-mee KWAHL-keh ahl-BEHR-goh?
We are staying at the hotel "XZ".	**Ci siamo fermati nell'albergo "XZ".**	chee SYAH-moh fehr-MAH-tee nehl-lahl-BEHR-goh "XZ"
Have you already booked the hotel?	**Hai già prenotato l'albergo?**	ahy JYAH preh-noh-TAH-toh lahl-BEHR-goh?

bed and breakfast
il bed and breakfast
eel bed and breakfast

single bed
il letto singolo
eel-LEHT-toh-SEEN-goh-loh

double bed
il letto matrimoniale
eel LEHT-toh mah-tree-moh-NYAH-leh

floor
il piano
eel PYAH-noh

front desk / reception
la reception
lah reception

hotel manager
la direttrice dell'albergo
lah dee-reht-TREE-cheh dehl-lahl-BEHR-goh

indoor pool
la piscina coperta
lah pee-SHEE-nah koh-PEHR-tah

key
la chiave
lah KYAH-veh

kitchenette
il cucinino
eel koo-chee-NEE-noh

luggage cart
il carrello per i bagagli
eel kahr-REHL-loh pehr ee bah-GAH-lyee

towels
gli asciugamani
lee ah-shyoo-gah-MAH-nee

room service
il servizio in camera
eel sehr-VEE-tsyoh een KAH-meh-rah

lobby
l'atrio
LAH-tryoh

wake-up call
il servizio sveglia
eel sehr-VEE-tsyoh ZVEH-lyah

reservation
la prenotazione
lah preh-noh-tah-TSYOH-neh

guest
l'ospite
LOH-spee-teh

check-in	**il check-in**	eel check-in
check-out	**il check-out**	eel check-out
complimentary breakfast	**la colazione inclusa nel prezzo**	lah koh-lah-TSYOH-neh een-KLOO-zah nehl PREH-tstsoh
king-size bed	**il letto king-size**	eel LEHT-toh king-size
late charge	**la penale per il ritardo**	lah peh-NAH-leh pehr eel ree-TAHR-doh
full	**pieno / completo**	PYEH-noh / kohm-PLEH-toh
parking pass	**il pass parcheggio**	eel pahss pahr-KEH-djdjyoh
pay-per-view movie	**il film in pay-per-view**	eel feelm een pay-per-view
queen-size bed	**il letto queen-size**	eel LEHT-toh queen-size
rate	**il prezzo**	eel PREH-tstsoh
vacancy	**la disponibilità**	lah dees-poh-nee-bee-lee-TAH

city-centre / downtown
il centro città
eel CHEHN-troh cheet-TAH

capital
la capitale
lah kah-pee-TAH-leh

centre
il centro
eel CHEHN-troh

district
il quartiere
eel kwar-TYEH-reh

industrial zone
la zona industriale
lah DZOH-nah een-doo-STRYAH-leh

city
la città
lah cheet-TAH

metropolis
la metropoli
lah meh-TROH-poh-lee

region
la regione
lah reh-JYOH-neh

seaside resort
la località balneare
lah loh-kah-lee-TAH
bahl-neh-AH-reh

old town
il centro storico
eel CHEHN-troh STOH-ree-koh

ski resort
la stazione sciistica
lah stah-TSYOH-neh shee-EE-stee-kah

small town
la piccola città
la PEEK-kohl-lah cheet-TAH

suburb
la periferia
lah peh-ree-feh-REE-yah

village
il villaggio
eel veel-LAH-djajyoh

winter resort
la località invernale
lah loh-kah-lee-TAH een-vehr-NAH-leh

alley
il vialetto
eel vyah-LEHT-toh

boulevard
il viale
eel VYAH-leh

motorway
l'autostrada
low-toh-STRAH-dah

toll road
la strada a pedaggio
lah STRAH-dah ah peh-DAH-djdjyoh

country road
la strada extraurbana
lah STRAH-dah ehks-trah-oor-BAH-nah

street
la via
lah VEE-yah

cycle lane
la pista ciclabile
lah PEES-tah chee-KLAH-bee-leh

cycle path
il percorso ciclabile
eel pehr-KOHR-soh chee-KLAH-bee-leh

crossroads / intersection
l'incrocio
leen-KROH-chyoh

traffic lights
il semaforo
eel seh-MAH-foh-roh

red light
il semaforo rosso
eel seh-MAH-foh-roh ROHS-soh

orange light
il semaforo giallo
eel seh-MAH-foh-roh JYAHL-loh

green light
il semaforo verde
eel seh-MAH-foh-roh VEHR-deh

roundabout
la rotonda
lah roh-TOHN-dah

pedestrian crossing
il passaggio pedonale
eel pahs-SAH-djdjyoh peh-doh-NAH-leh

pavement
il marciapiede
eel mahr-chyah-PYEH-deh

bridge
il ponte
eel POHN-teh

footbridge
il ponte pedonale
eel POHN-teh peh-doh-NAH-leh

overpass
la cavalcavia
lah kah-vahl-kah-VEE-yah

underpass
il sottopassaggio
eel soht-toh-pahs-SAH-djdjyoh

tunnel
il tunnel
eel TOON-nehl

road
la strada
lah STRAH-dah

street corner
l'angolo di strada
LAHN-goh-loh dee STRAH-dah

one-way street
la strada a senso unico
lah STRAH-dah ah SEHN-soh OO-nee-koh

avenue	**il viale**	eel VYAH-leh
four-lane road	**la strada a quattro corsie**	lah STRAH-dah a KWAHT-troh kohr-SEE-yeh
main road	**la strada principale**	lah STRAH-dah preen-chee-PAH-leh
side street	**la traversa**	lah trah-VEHR-sah
expressway	**l'autostrada**	low-toh-STRAH-dah
two-lane road	**la strada a due corsie**	lah STRAH-dah ah DOO-weh kohr-SEE-yeh
fast lane	**la corsia di sorpasso**	lah kohr-SEE-yah dee sohr-PAHS-soh
left lane	**la corsia di sinistra**	lah kohr-SEE-yah dee see-NEE-strah
right lane	**la corsia di destra**	lah kohr-SEE-yah dee DEH-strah
breakdown lane	**la corsia d'emergenza**	lah kohr-SEE-yah deh-mehr-JEHN-tsah

attractions
le attrazioni
leh aht-trah-TSYOH-nee

casino
il casinò
eel kah-zee-NOH

guide book
la guida
lah GWEE-dah

park
il parco
eel PAHR-koh

guided tour
la visita guidata
lah VEE-zee-tah gwee-DAH-tah

information
l'informazione
leen-fohr-mah-TSYOH-neh

itinerary
il percorso
eel pehr-KOHR-soh

ruins
le rovine
leh roh-VEE-neh

monument
il monumento
eel moh-noo-MEHN-toh

museum
il museo
eel moo-ZEH-oh

national park
il parco nazionale
eel PAHR-koh nah-tsyoh-NAH-leh

sightseeing
il giro turistico
eel JEE-roh too-REES-tee-koh

souvenirs
i souvenir
ee soo-veh-NEER

tour bus
l'autobus turistico
LOW-toh-boos too-REES-tee-koh

tourist
il turista *m* / la turista *f*
eel too-REE-stah / lah too-REE-stah

entrance fee / price	**il biglietto d'ingresso**	eel bee-LYEHT-toh deen-GREHS-soh
to buy a souvenir	**comprare un souvenir**	kohm-PRAH-reh oon soo-veh-NEER
to do a tour	**fare un giro**	FAH-reh oon JEE-roh
tour guide	**la guida turistica**	lah GWEE-dah too-REES-tee-kah

airport
l'aeroporto
lah-eh-roh-POHR-toh

bank
la banca
lah BAHN-kah

bus stop
la fermata dell'autobus
lah fehr-MAH-tah dehl-LOW-toh-boos

church
la chiesa
lah KYEH-zah

cinema
il cinema
eel CHEE-neh-mah

city / town hall
il municipio
eel moo-nee-CHEE-pyoh

department store
il grande magazzino
eel GRAHN-deh mah-gah-DZDZEE-noh

factory
la fabbrica
lah FAHB-bree-kah

fire station
la caserma dei vigili del fuoco
lah kah-ZEHR-mah day VEE-jee-lee dehl
FWOH-koh

hospital
l'ospedale
lohs-peh-DAH-leh

hotel
l'albergo
lahl-BEHR-goh

library
la libreria
lah lee-breh-REE-yah

theatre
il teatro
eel teh-AH-troh

museum
il museo
eel moo-ZEH-oh

parking area
il parcheggio
eel pahr-KEH-djdjyoh

playground
il parco giochi
eel PAHR-koh JYOH-kee

police station
la stazione di polizia
lah stah-TSYOH-neh dee poh-lee-TSEE-yah

post office
l'ufficio postale
loof-FEE-chyoh poh-STAH-leh

prison
la prigione / il carcere
lah pree-JYOH-neh / eel KAHR-cheh-reh

restaurant
il ristorante
eel rees-toh-RAHN-teh

school
la scuola
lah SKWOH-lah

taxi stand
il posteggio dei tassì
eel poh-STEH-djdjyoh day tahs-SEE

harbour
il porto
eel POHR-toh

square
la piazza
lah PYAH-tstsah

supermarket
il supermercato
eel soo-pehr-mehr-KAH-toh

railway station
la stazione ferroviaria
lah stah-TSYOH-neh fehr-roh-VYAH-ryah

| How do I get to the railway station? | **Come arrivare alla stazione ferroviaria?** | KOH-meh ahr-ree-VAH-reh AHL-lah stah-TSYOH-neh fehr-roh-VYAH-ryah? |
| Where can I find a taxi? | **Dove trovo un tassi?** | DOV-veh TROH voh oon tahs SEE? |

snorkel
il boccaglio
eel bohk-KAH-lyoh

diving mask
la maschera da sub
lah MAH-skeh-rah dah SOOB

swimming goggles
gli occhialini
lee ohk-kyah-LEE-nee

sunglasses
gli occhiali da sole
lee ohk-KYAH-lee dah SOH-leh

beach ball
il pallone da spiaggia
eel pahl-LOH-neh dah
SPYAH-djdjyah

sunscreen
la crema solare
lah KREH-mah soh-LAH-reh

hat
il cappello
eel kahp-PEHL-loh

beach towel
il telo da mare
eel TEH-loh dah MAH-reh

beach
la spiaggia
lah SPYAH-djdjyah

sun lounger
Il lettino prendisole
eel leht-TEE-noh prehn-dee-SOH-leh

swimming cap	**la cuffia**	lah COOF-fyah
bikini	**il bikini**	eel bee-KEE-nee
swimming costume	**il costume da bagno**	eel kohs-TOO-meh dah BAH-nyoh
to sunbathe	**prendere il sole**	PREHN-deh-reh eel SOH-leh
to swim	**nuotare**	nwoh-TAH-reh

HEALTH

medicines
le medicine
leh meh-dee-CHEE-neh

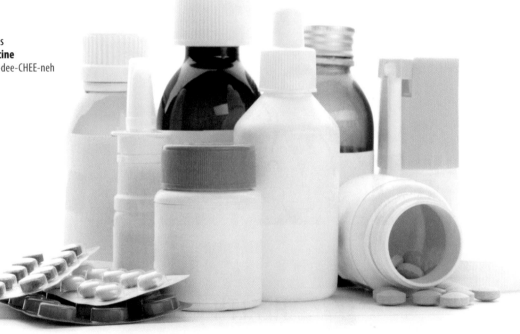

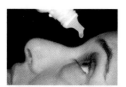

eye drops
il collirio
eel kohl-LEE-ryoh

painkiller
l'antidolorifico
lahn-tee-doh-loh-REE-fee-koh

syrup
lo sciroppo
loh shee-ROHP-poh

to take medicine
prendere medicine
PREHN-deh-reh meh-dee-CHEE-neh

shot / injection
la puntura / l'iniezione
lah poon-TOO-rah /
lee-nyeh-TSYOH-neh

sleeping pill
il sonnifero
eel sohn-NEE-feh-roh

plaster
il cerotto
eel chehr-ROHT-toh

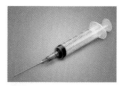

syringe
la siringa
lah see-REEN-gah

gauze
la garza
lah GAHR-tsah

pill
la pillola
lah PEEL-loh-lah

tablet
la compressa
lah kohm-PREHS-sah

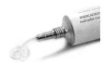

ointment
l'unguento
loon-GWEHN-toh

155

hospital
l'ospedale
lohs-peh-DAH-leh

nurse
l'infermiere *m* / l'infermiera *f*
leen-fehr-MYEH-reh / leen-fehr-MYEH-rah

doctor / physician
il dottore *m* / la dottoressa *f* / il medico *m* / *f*
eel doht-TOH-reh / lah doht-toh-REHS-sah /
eel MEH-dee-koh

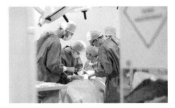

operation / surgery
l'operazione / l'intervento chirurgico
loh-peh-rah-TSYOH-neh /
leen-tehr-VEHN-toh kee-ROOR-jee-koh

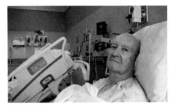

patient
il paziente *m* / la paziente *f*
eel pah-TSYEHN-teh / lah pah-TSYEHN-teh

waiting room
la sala d'attesa
lah SAH-lah daht-TEH-zah

check-up	**il controllo**	eel kohn-TROHL-loh	prescription	**la prescrizione**	lah preh-skree-TSYOH-neh
diagnosis	**la diagnosi**	lah DYAH-nyoh-zee	specialist	**lo specialista**	loh-speh-chyah-LEE-stah
pharmacy / chemist's	**la farmacia**	lah fahr-mah-CHEE-yah	treatment	**la terapia**	lah teh-rah-PEE-yah

allergist
l'allergologo *m* / **l'allergologa** *f*
lahl-lehr-GOH-loh-goh /
lahl-lehr-GOH-loh-gah

dentist
il dentista *m* / **la dentista** *f*
eel dehn-TEE-stah /
lah dehn-TEE-stah

gynecologist
il ginecologo *m* / **la ginecologa** *f*
eel gee-neh-KOH-loh-goh /
lah gee-neh-KOH-loh-gah

pediatrician
il pediatra *m* / **la pediatra** *f*
eel peh-DYAH-trah /
lah peh-DYAH-trah

physiotherapist
il fisioterapista *m* /
la fisioterapista *f*
eel fee-zyoh-teh-rah-PEES-tah /
lah fee-zyoh-teh-rah-PEES-tah

midwife
l'ostetrica
lohs-TEH-tree-kah

ophthalmologist
l'oculista
loh-koo-LEE-stah

surgeon
il chirurgo *m* / **la chirurga** *f*
eel kee-ROOR-goh /
lah kee-ROOR-gah

anaesthesiologist	**l'anestesista**	lah-neh-steh-ZEE-stah
cardiologist	**il cardiologo** *m* / **la cardiologa** *f*	eel kahr-DYOH-loh-goh / lah kahr-DYOH-loh-gah
dermatologist	**il dermatologo** *m* / **la dermatologa** *f*	eel dehr-mah-TOH-loh-goh / la dehr-mah-TOH-loh-gah
neurologist	**il neurologo** *m* / **la neurologa** *f*	eel nehw-ROH-loh-goh / lah nehw-ROH-loh-gah
psychiatrist	**lo psichiatra** *m* / **la psichiatra** *f*	loh psee-KYAH-trah / lah psee-KYAH-trah
radiologist	**il radiologo** *m* / **la radiologa** *f*	eel rah-DYOH-loh-goh / lah rah-DYOH-loh-gah

to feel good
sentirsi bene
sehn-TEER-see BEH-neh

to catch a cold
prendere un raffreddore
PREHN-deh-reh oon rahf-frehd-DOH-reh

to have a cold
avere un raffreddore
ah-VEH-reh oon rahf-frehd-DOH-reh

to sneeze
starnutire
stahr-noo-TEE-reh

to cough
tossire
tohs-SEE-reh

to blow one's nose
soffiarsi il naso
sohf-FYAHR-see eel NAH-zoh

to feel sick
sentirsi male
sehn-TEER-see MAH-leh

to faint
svenire
zveh-NEE-reh

to pass out
svenire
zveh-NEE-reh

to be tired
essere stanco
EHS-seh-reh STAHN-koh

to be exhausted
essere esausto
EHS-seh-reh eh-ZOW-stoh

to have back pain
avere mal di schiena
ah-VEH-reh mahl dee SKYEH-nah

to have earache
avere mal d'orecchi
ah-VEH-reh mahl doh-REHK-kee

to have a headache
avere mal di testa
ah-VEH-reh mahl dee TEH-stah

to have a sore throat
avere mal di gola
ah-VEH-reh mahl dee GOH-lah

to have toothache
avere mal di denti
ah-VEH-reh mahl dee DEHN-tee

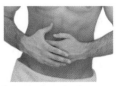

to have a stomach ache
avere mal di stomaco
ah-VEH-reh mahl dee STOH-mah-koh

to have a temperature
avere la febbre
ah-VEH-reh lah FEHB-breh

to have diarrhoea
avere la diarrea
ah-VEH-reh lah diahr-REH-ah

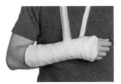

to break an arm
rompere un braccio
ROHM-peh-reh oon BRAH-chchyoh

to be constipated
avere costipazione
ah-VEH-reh koh-stee-pah-TSYOH-neh

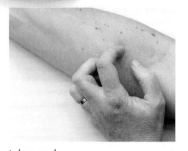

to have a rash
avere un'eruzione cutanea
ah-VEH-reh oon-eh-roo-TSYOH-neh coo-TAH-neh-ah

to be allergic to
essere allergico a
EHS-seh-reh ahl-LEHR-jee-koh ah

to vomit
vomitare
voh-mee-TAH-reh

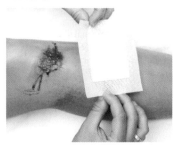

to hurt
fare male
FAH-reh MAH-leh

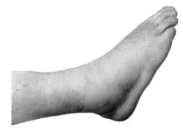

to swell
gonfiarsi
gohn-FYAHR-see

to suffer from
soffrire di qualcosa
sohf-FREE-reh dee kwahl-KOH-zah

chicken pox
la varicella
lah vah-ree-CHEHL-lah

runny nose
il naso che cola
eel NAH-zoh keh KOH-lah

heart attack
l'infarto
leen-FAHR-toh

cough
la tosse
lah TOHS-seh

diarrhoea
la diarrea
lah dyahr-REH-ah

fever
la febbre
lah FEHB-breh

headache
il mal di testa
eel mahl dee TEH-stah

injury
la lesione
lah leh-ZYOH-neh

sore throat
la gola infiammata
lah GOH-lah een-fyahm-
MAH-tah

asthma
l'asma
LAHS-mah

flu
l'influenza
leen-floo-EHN-tsah

health
la salute
lah sah-LOO-teh

hepatitis
l'epatite
leh-pah-TEE-teh

heart disease
la cardiopatia
lah kahr-dyoh-pah-TEE-yah

stomach ache
il mal di stomaco
eel mahl dee STOH-mah-koh

mouth ulcer
l'ulcera della bocca
LOOL-cheh-rah DEHL-lah
BOHK-kah

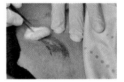

wound
la ferita
lah feh-REE-tah

common cold	**il raffreddore comune**	eel rahf-frehd-DOH-reh koh-MOO-neh
fracture	**la frattura**	lah fraht-TOO-rah
illness	**la malattia**	lah mah-laht-TEE-yah
mumps	**gli orecchioni**	lee oh-rehk-KYOH-nee

pain	**il dolore**	eel doh-LOH-reh
painful	**doloroso**	doh-loh-ROH-zoh
painless	**indolore**	een-doh-LOH-reh
to be ill	**essere malato**	EHS-seh-reh mah-LAH-toh

emergency number
il numero di emergenza
eel NOO-meh-roh dee eh-mehr-JEHN-tsah

firefighter
il pompiere / il vigile del fuoco
eel pohm-PYEH-reh / eel VEE-jee-leh dehl
FWOH-koh

policeman
il poliziotto
eel poh-lee-TSYOHT-toh

fire engine
l'autopompa
low-toh-POHM-pah

police car
l'auto della polizia
LOW-toh DEHL-lah poh-lee-TSEE-yah

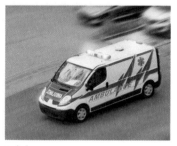

ambulance
l'ambulanza
lahm-boo-LAHN-tsah

accident
l'incidente
leen-chee-DEHN-teh

paramedics
i paramedici
ee pah-rah-MEH-dee-chee

emergency
l'emergenza
leh-mehr-JEHN-tsah

fire
il fuoco
eel FWUH-koh

patient
il paziente *m* / **la paziente** *f*
eel pahts-YEHN-teh / lah pahts-YEHN-teh

police
la polizia
lah poh-lee-TSEE-yah

SPORT

badminton racket
la racchetta da badminton
lah rahk-KEHT-tah dah BAHD-meen-tohn

ball
la palla
lah PAHL-lah

baseball
la palla da baseball
lah PAHL-lah dah baseball

bicycle
la bicicletta
lah bee-chee-KLEHT-tah

bowling ball
la palla da bowling
lah PAHL-lah dah BOO-leeng

cap
il berretto
eel behr-REHT-toh

football
il pallone da calcio
eel pahl-LOH-neh dah KAHL-chyoh

glove
il guanto
eel GWAHN-toh

net
la rete
lah REH-teh

goggles
gli occhiali
lee ohk-KYAH-lee

golf ball
la pallina da golf
lah pahl-LEE-nah dah golf

helmet
il casco
eel KAHS-koh

goal
la porta
lah POHR-tah

hockey puck
il disco da hockey
eel DEES-koh dah OH-kay

hockey stick
la mazza da hockey
lah MAH-dzdzah dah OH-kay

saddle
la sella
lah SEHL-lah

ice-skates
i pattini (da ghiaccio)
ee PAHT-tee-nee (dah GYAH-chchyoh)

lane
la corsia
lah kohr-SEE-yah

skates
i pattini
ee PAHT-tee-nee

ski poles
i bastoncini da sci
ee bahs-tohn-CHEE-nee dah shee

167

skis
gli sci
lee shee

snowboard
lo snowboard
lo ZNOW-bohrd

surfboard
la tavola da surf
lah TAH-voh-lah dah sehrf

squash racket
la racchetta da squash
lah rahk-KEHT-tah dah squash

swimming costume
il costume da bagno
eel kohs-TOO-meh dah BAH-nyoh

tennis ball
la palla da tennis
lah PAHL-lah dah TEHN-nees

tennis racket
la racchetta da tennis
lah rahk-KEHT-tah dah TEHN-nees

volleyball
il pallone da pallavolo
eel pahl-LOH-neh dah
pahl-lah-VOH-loh

weights
i pesi
ee PEH-zee

baseball
il baseball
eel baseball

bowling
il bowling
eel BOO-leeng

football
il calcio
eel KAHL-chyoh

hiking
l'escursionismo
leh-skoor-syoh-NEE-zmoh

hockey
l'hockey
LOH-key

cycling
il ciclismo
eel chee-KLEE-zmoh

horseriding
l'equitazione
leh-kwee-tah-TSYOH-neh

running
la corsa
lah KOHR-sah

skating
il pattinaggio
eel paht-tee-NAH-djdjyoh

skiing
gli sci
lee shee

swimming
il nuoto
eel NWOH-toh

tennis
il tennis
eel TEHN-nees

volleyball
la pallavolo
lah pahl-lah-VOH-loh

weightlifting
il sollevamento pesi
eel sohl-leh-vah-MEHN-to PEH-zee

basketball court
il campo da basket
eel KAHM-poh dah BAH-skeht

boxing ring
il ring
eel ring

fitness centre
il centro fitness
eel CHEHN-troh fitness

football pitch
il campo da calcio
eel KAHM-poh dah KAHL-chyoh

golf course
il campo da golf
eel KAHM-poh dah golf

football ground
il campo da calcio
eel KAHM-poh dah KAHL-chyoh

golf club
il golf club
eel golf club

gym
la palestra
lah pah-LEH-strah

playground
il parco giochi
eel PAHR-koh JYOH-kee

racecourse
l'ippodromo
leep-POH-droh-moh

racing track
la pista
lah PEE-stah

recreation area
l'area di ricreazione
LAH-reh-ah dee ree-kreh-ah-TSYOH-neh

skating rink
la pista di pattinaggio
lah PEE-stah dee paht-tee-
NAH-djdjyoh

sports ground
il campo sportivo
eel KAHM-poh spohr-TEE-voh

stadium
lo stadio
loh STAH-dyoh

swimming pool
la piscina
lah pee-SHEE-nah

tennis club
il tennis club
eel TEHN-nees club

tennis court
il campo da tennis
eel KAHM-poh dah TEHN-nees

NATURE

landscape
il paesaggio
eel pah-eh-SAH-djdjyoh

bay
la baia
lah BAH-yah

beach
la spiaggia
lah SPYAH-djdjyah

cave
la grotta
lah GROHT-tah

stream
il torrente
eel tohr-REHN-teh

desert
il deserto
eel deh-ZEHR-toh

forest / woods
la foresta / il bosco
lah foh-REH-stah / eel BOH-skoh

hill
la collina
lah kohl-LEE-nah

earth
la terra
lah TEHR-rah

island
l'isola
LEE-zoh-lah

lake
il lago
eel LAH-goh

mountain
la montagna
lah mohn-TAH-nyah

ocean
l'oceano
loh-CHEH-ah-noh

peak
la cima
lah CHEE-mah

plain
la pianura
lah pyah-NOO-rah

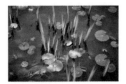

pond
lo stagno
loh STAH-nyoh

river
il fiume
eel FYOO-meh

sea
il mare
eel MAH-reh

brook
la corrente
lah kohr-REHN-teh

swamp
la palude
lah pah-LOO-deh

valley
la valle
lah VAHL-leh

waterfall
la cascata
lah kahs-KAH-tah

weather
il tempo
eel TEHM-poh

What's the weather like?	Com'è il tempo?	koh-MEH eel TEHM-poh?
What's the forecast for tomorrow?	**Quali sono le previsioni per domani?**	KWAH-lee SOH-no leh preh-vee-ZYOH-nee pehr doh-MAH-nee?

blizzard
la tormenta
lah tohr-MEHN-tah

cold
freddo
FREHD-doh

drizzle
la pioggerella
lah pyoh-djdjeh-REHL-lah

flood
l'alluvione
lahl-loo-VYOH-neh

frost
il gelo
eel JEH-loh

humidity
l'umidità
loo-mee-dee-TAH

Celsius
Centigrado
chen-TEE-grah-doh

cyclone
il ciclone
eel chee-KLOH-neh

dry
secco
SEHK-koh

fog
la nebbia
lah NEHB-byah

hail
la grandine
lah GRAHN-dee-neh

hurricane
l'uragano
loo-rah-GAH-noh

cloud
la nuvola
lah NOO-voh-lah

degree
il grado
eel GRAH-doh

dry season
la stagione secca
lah stah-DJYOH-neh SEHK-kah

forecast
la previsione
lah preh-vee-ZYOH-neh

heat
il calore
eel kah-LOH-reh

ice
il ghiaccio
eel GHYAH-chchyoh

cloudy
nuvoloso
noo-voh-LOH-zoh

dew
la rugiada
lah roo-JYAH-dah

Fahrenheit
Fahrenheit
fah-rehn-AHYT

freeze
gelare
jeh-LAH-reh

hot
caldo
KAHL-doh

lightning
il fulmine
eel FOOL-mee-neh

rain
la pioggia
lah PYOH-djdjyah

 rainy season
la stagione delle piogge
lah stah-DJYOH-neh
DEHL-leh PYOH-djdjeh

 snowy
nevoso
neh-VOH-zoh

 temperature
la temperatura
lah tehm-peh-rah-TOO-rah

 tsunami
il tsunami
eel tsoo-NAH-mee

 rainstorm
il temporale
eel tehm-poh-RAH-leh

 sleet
il nevischio
eel neh-VEES-kyoh

 storm
la tempesta
lah tehm-PEH-stah

 thunder
il tuono
eel TWOH-noh

 typhoon
il tifone
eel tee-FOH-neh

 windy
ventoso
vehn-TOH-zoh

 rainbow
l'arcobaleno
lahr-koh-bah-LEH-noh

 snow
la neve
lah NEH-veh

 sun
il sole
eel SOH-leh

 thunderstorm
il temporale
eel tehm-poh-RAH-leh

 warm
caldo
KAHL-doh

 rainy
piovoso
pyoh-VOH-zoh

 snowstorm
la bufera di neve
lah boo-FEH-rah dee
NEH-veh

 sunny
soleggiato
soh-leh-DJDJYAH-toh

 tornado
il tornado
eel tohr-NAH-doh

 wind
il vento
eel VEHN-toh

aquarium
l'acquario
lah-KWAH-ryoh

cage
la gabbia
lah GAHB-byah

pet owner
la proprietaria dell'animale
lah proh-pryeh-TAH-ryah dehl-lah-nee-MAH-leh

bird
l'uccello
loo-CHCHEHL-loh

dog
il cane
eel KAH-neh

canary
il canarino
eel kah-nah-REE-noh

cat
il gatto
eel GAHT-toh

pet shop
il negozio di animali
eel neh-GOH-tsyoh dee ah-nee-MAH-lee

fish
il pesce
eel PEH-sheh

gecko
il geco
eel JEH-koh

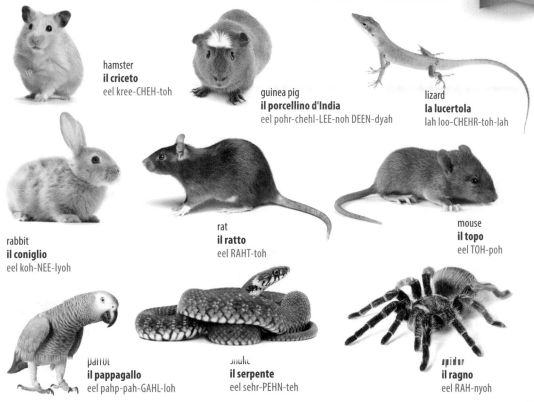

hamster
il criceto
eel kree-CHEH-toh

guinea pig
il porcellino d'India
eel pohr-chehl-LEE-noh DEEN-dyah

lizard
la lucertola
lah loo-CHEHR-toh-lah

rabbit
il coniglio
eel koh-NEE-lyoh

rat
il ratto
eel RAHT-toh

mouse
il topo
eel TOH-poh

parrot
il pappagallo
eel pahp-pah-GAHL-loh

snake
il serpente
eel sehr-PEHN-teh

spider
il ragno
eel RAH-nyoh

cow
la mucca
lah MOOK-kah

chicken
il pollo
eel POHL-loh

donkey
l'asino
LAH-zee-noh

goose
l'oca
LOH-kah

goat
la capra
lah KAH-prah

horse
il cavallo
eel kah-VAHL-loh

sheep
la pecora
lah PEH-koh-rah

duck
l'anatra
LAH-nah-trah

rabbit
il coniglio
eel koh-NEE-lyoh

pig
il maiale
eel mah-YAH-leh

turkey
il tacchino
eel tahk-KEE-noh

giraffe
la giraffa
lah jee-RAHF-fah

elephant
l'elefante
leh-leh-FAHN-teh

jaguar
il giaguaro
eel jyah-GWAH-roh

tiger
la tigre
lah TEE-greh

lion
il leone
eel leh-OH-neh

leopard
il leopardo
eel leh-oh-PAHR-doh

puma
la puma
lah POO-mah

hippopotamus
l'ippopotamo
leep-poh-POH-
tah-moh

monkey
la scimmia
lah SHEEM-myah

chimpanzee
lo scimpanzé
loh sheem-pahn-DZEH

ostrich
lo struzzo
loh STROO-tstshoh

sloth
il bradipo
eel BRAH-dee-poh

rhinoceros
il rinoceronte
eel ree-noh-cheh-
ROHN-teh

armadillo
l'armadillo
lahr-mah-DEEL-loh

bear
l'orso
LOHR-soh

iguana
l'iguana
lee-GWAH-nah

kangaroo
il canguro
eel kahn-GOO-roh

zebra
la zebra
lah DZEH-brah

hyena
la iena
lah YEH-nah

seal
la foca
lah FOH-kah

gazelle
la gazzella
lah gah-DZDZEHL-lah

antelope
l'antilope
lahn-TEE-loh-peh

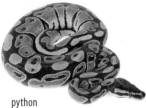

python
il pitone
eel pee-TOH-neh

water buffalo
il bufalo d'acqua
eel BOO-fah-loh DAH-kwah

boar
il cinghiale
eel cheen-GYAH-leh

cobra
il cobra
eel KOH-brah

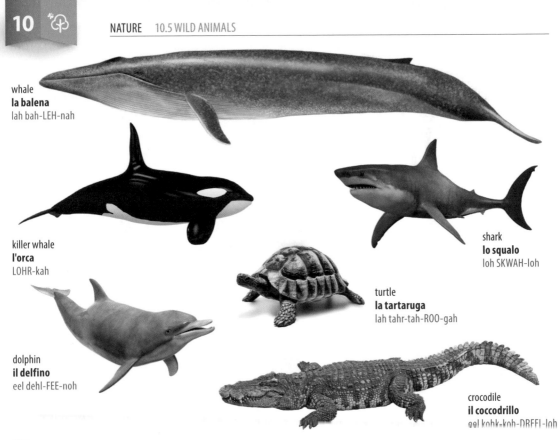

whale
la balena
lah bah-LEH-nah

killer whale
l'orca
LOHR-kah

shark
lo squalo
loh SKWAH-loh

dolphin
il delfino
eel dehl-FEE-noh

turtle
la tartaruga
lah tahr-tah-ROO-gah

crocodile
il coccodrillo
eel kohk-koh-DREEL-loh

 SHOPPING AND SERVICES

grocery store
il negozio di alimentari
eel neh-GOH-tsyoh dee ah-lee-mehn-TAH-ree

flower market
il mercato dei fiori
eel mehr-KAH-toh day FYOH-ree

flea market
il mercatino
eel mehr-kah-TEE-noh

bazaar
il bazar
eel bah-DZAHR

computer shop
il negozio di informatica
eel neh-GOH-tsyoh dee een-fohr-MAH-tee-kah

farmers' market
il mercato dei prodotti agricoli
eel mehr-KAH-toh day proh-DOHT-tee ah-GREE-koh-lee

bookshop
la libreria
lah lee-breh-REE-ya

corner shop
il negozio di quartiere
eel neh-GOH-tsyoh dee kwahr-TYEH-reh

bakery
il panificio
eel pah-nee-FEE-chyoh

fruit stall
la bancarella di frutta
lah bahn-kah-REHL-lah dee FROOT-tah

market
il mercato
eel mehr-KAH-toh

newsagent
il giornalaio / l'edicola
eel jyohr-nah-LAH-yoh / leh-DEE-koh-lah

shoe shop
il negozio di scarpe
eel neh-GOH-tsyoh dee SKAHR-peh

street vendor
il venditore ambulante
eel vehn-dee-TOH-reh ahm-boo-LAHN-teh

supermarket
il supermercato
eel soo-pehr-mehr-KAH-toh

department store	**il grande magazzino**	eel GRAHN-deh mah-gah-DZDZEE-noh
market	**il mercato**	eel mehr-KAH-toh
shopping centre	**il centro commerciale**	eel CHEHN-troh kohm-mehr-CHYAH-leh

reduction
i saldi
ee SAHL-dee

queue
la fila
lah FEE-lah

receipt
lo scontrino
loh skohn-TREE-noh

checkout / till checkout
la cassa
lah KAHS-sah

customer
il cliente *m* / la cliente *f*
eel klee-YEHN-teh / lah klee-YEHN-teh

cashier
il cassiere *m* / la cassiera *f*
eel kahs-SYEH-reh /
lah kahs-SYEH-rah

conveyor belt
il nastro trasportatore
eel NAH-stroh trahs-pohr-
tah-TOH-reh

price
il prezzo
eel PREH-tstsoh

shopping bag
la borsa per la spesa
lah BOHR-sah pehr lah SPEH-zah

shopping list
la lista della spesa
lah LEES-tah DEHL-lah SPEH-zah

shopping basket
il cestino
eel cheh-STEE-noh

trolley
il carrello
eel kahr-REHL-loh

bill for	**il conto per**	eel KOHN-toh pehr
Can I help you?	**Posso aiutare?**	POHS-soh ah-yoo-TAH-reh?
goods	**i merci**	ee MEHR-chee
shopper	**l'acquirente**	lah-kwee-REHN-teh
to cost	**costare**	koh-STAH-reh
to get a great bargain	**ottenere un ottimo affare**	oht-teh-NEH-re oon OHT-tee-moh ahf-FAH-reh
to purchase	**acquistare**	ah-kwee-STAH-reh
to queue	**fare la fila**	FAH-reh lah FEE-lah

belt
la cintura
lah cheen-TOO-rah

boots
gli scarponcini
lee skahr-pohn-CHEE-nee

coat
il cappotto
eel kahp-POHT-toh

raincoat
l'impermeabile
leem-pehr-meh-AH-bee-leh

gloves
i guanti
ee GWAHN-tee

hat
il cappello
eel kahp-PEHL-loh

jeans
i jeans
ee jeans

pyjamas
il pigiama
eel pee-JYAH-mah

jacket
la giacca
lah JYAHK-kah

shoes
le scarpe
leh SKAHR-peh

jumper
il maglione
eel mah-LYOH-neh

scarf
la sciarpa
lah SHYAR-pah

underwear
la biancheria intima
lah byahn-keh-REE-yah EEN-tee-mah

tie
la cravatta
lah krah-VAHT-tah

sweatshirt
la felpa
lah FEHL-pah

briefs
gli slip
lee zleep

shirt
la camicia
lah kah-MEE-chyah

trousers
i pantaloni
ee pahn-tah-LOH-nee

t-shirt
la maglietta
lah mah-LYEHT-tah

socks
i calzini
ee kahl-TSEE-nee

undershirt
la canotta
lah kah-NOHT-tah

slippers
le pantofole
leh pahn-TOH-foh-leh

suit
il completo
eel kohm-PLEH-toh

He has a hat on.	**Lui porta un cappello.**	LOO-yee POHR-tah oon kahp-PEHL-loh
These briefs are the right size.	**Questi slip sono della taglia giusta.**	KWEHS-tee zleep SOH-noh DEHL-lah TAH-lyah JYOO-stah
What did he have on?	**Che cosa ha indossato?**	keh KOH-zah ah een-dohs-SAH-toh?
I want these boxer shorts in a size 42.	**Vorrei questi boxer in taglia 42.**	vohr-RAY KWEHS-tee BOH-ksehr een TAH-lyah kwah-RAHN-tah DOO-weh

boots
gli stivali
lee stee-VAH-lee

jacket
la giacca
lah JYAHK-kah

gloves
i guanti
ee GWAHN-tee

hat
il cappello
eel kahp-PEHL-loh

jeans
i jeans
ee jeans

raincoat
l'impermeabile
leem-pehr-meh-
AH-bee-leh

pyjamas
il pigiama
eel pee-JYAH-mah

coat
il cappotto
eel kahp-POHT-toh

belt
la cintura
lah cheen-TOO-rah

195

scarf
la sciarpa
lah SHYAHR-pah

jumper
il maglione
eel mah-LYOH-neh

pants
le mutande
leh moo-TAHN-deh

dress
il vestito
eel vehs-TEE-toh

skirt
la gonna
lah GOHN-nah

shoes
le scarpe
leh SKAHR-peh

sweatshirt
la felpa
lah FEHL-pah

socks
i calzini
ee kahl-TSEE-nee

shirt
la camicia
lah kah-MEE-chyah

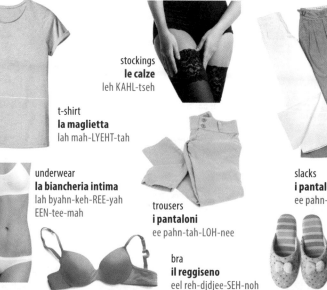

suit
il completo
eel kohm-PLEH-toh

stockings
le calze
leh KAHL-tseh

t-shirt
la maglietta
lah mah-LYEHT-tah

underwear
la biancheria intima
lah byahn-keh-REE-yah EEN-tee-mah

trousers
i pantaloni
ee pahn-tah-LOH-nee

slacks
i pantaloni
ee pahn-tah-LOH-nee

bra
il reggiseno
eel reh-djdjee-SEH-noh

slippers
le pantofole
leh pahn-TOH-foh-leh

She has a hat on.	**Lei porta un cappello.**	lay POHR-tah oon kahp-PEHL-loh
The dress looks nice on you.	**Il vestito ti sta bene.**	eel vehs-TEE-toh tee stah BEH-neh
What did she have on?	**Che cosa lei ha indossato?**	keh KOH-zah lay ah een-dohs-SAH-toh?
I want the boots in a size 38.	**Voglio gli stivali di numero 38.**	VOH-lyoh lee stee-VAH-lee dee NOO-meh-roh trehnt-OHT-toh

bicycle repair shop
il negozio di biciclette
eel neh-GOH-tsyoh dee bee-chee-KLEHT-teh

barber shop
il barbiere
eel bahr-BYEH-reh

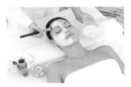

beauty salon
il salone di bellezza
eel sah-LOH-neh dee behl-LEH-tstsah

car repair shop
il meccanico
eel mehk-KAH-nee-koh

watchmaker
l'orologiaio
loh-roh-loh-JYAH-yoh

dry cleaners
la lavanderia
lah lah-vahn-deh-REE-yah

laundromat
la lavanderia a gettoni
lah lah-vahn-deh-REE-yah ah jeht-TOH-nee

locksmiths
la bottega del fabbro
lah boht-TEH-gah dehl FAHB-broh

petrol station
la stazione di servizio
lah stah-TSYOH-neh dee sehr-VEE-tsyoh

CULTURE AND MEDIA

blog
il blog
eel blog

to broadcast
trasmettere
trahs-MEHT-teh-reh

magazine
la rivista
lah ree-VEE-stah

newspaper
il giornale
eel jyohr-NAH-leh

radio
la radio
lah RAH-dyoh

television
la televisione
lah teh-leh-vee-SYOH-neh

news broadcast
il telegiornale
eel teh-leh-jyohr-NAH-leh

weather forecast
le previsioni meteo
leh preh-veez-YOH-nee meh-TEH-oh

blogosphere	**la blogosfera**	lah bloh-goh-SFEH-rah
mass media	**i mass media**	ee mass media
news	**le notizie**	leh noh-TEE-tsyeh
press	**la stampa**	lah STAHM-pah
tabloid	**il tabloid**	eel tah-BLOH-eed
programme	**il programma**	eel proh-GRAHM-mah
soap	**la soap opera**	lah sohwp OH-peh-rah
drama	**il dramma**	eel DRAHM-mah
series	**la serie**	lah SEHR-yeh
film	**il film**	eel feelm
documentary	**il documentario**	eel doh-koo-mehn-TAH-ryoh
music programme	**il programma musicale**	eel proh-GRAHM-mah moo-zee-KAH-leh
sports programme	**il programma sportivo**	eel proh-GRAHM-mah spohr-TEE-voh
talk show	**il talk show**	eel tohk shoh
episode	**l'episodio**	leh-pee-ZOH-dyoh
business news	**le informazioni economiche**	leh een-fohr-mah-TSYOH-nee eh-koh-NOH-mee-keh
sports report	**la cronaca sportiva**	lah KROH-nah-kah spohr-TEE-vah
book review	**la recensione del libro**	lah reh-chehn-SYOH-neh dehl LEE-broh
ad, advertisement	**la pubblicità**	lah poob-blee-chee-TAH

message
il messaggio
eel mehs-SAH-djdjyoh

address URL
l'indirizzo URL
leen-dee-REE-tstsoh oo EHR-reh EHL-leh

application / app
l'app
lahp

network
la rete
lah REH-teh

inbox	**la posta in arrivo**	lah POHS-tah een ahr-REE-voh
IP address	**l'indirizzo IP**	leen-dee-REE-tstsoh ee-pee
internet	**l'Internet**	LEEN-tehr-neht
website	**il sito web**	eel SEE-toh web
mail	**la posta**	lah POHS-tah
search engine	**il motore di ricerca**	eel moh-TOH-reh dee ree-CHEHR-kah
to search	**cercare**	chehr-KAH-reh
to share	**condividere**	kohn-dee-VEE-deh-reh
to log in	**connettersi**	kohn-NEHT-tehr-see

to send
inviare
een-vee-YAH-reh

login
il login
eel LOH-geen

to log out
disconnettersi
dees-kohn-NEHT-tehr-see

to upload	**caricare**	cah-ree-KAH-reh
to download	**scaricare**	skah-ree-KAH-reh
to tag	**contrassegnare**	kohn-trahs-seh-NYAH-reh
to comment	**commentare**	kohm-mehn-TAH-reh
to publish	**pubblicare**	poob-blee-KAH-reh
to contact	**contattare**	kohn-taht-TAH-reh
to receive	**ricevere**	ree-CHEH-veh-reh
to add	**aggiungere**	ah-DJDJYOON-jeh-reh

link
il collegamento
eel kohl-leh-gah-MEHN-toh

DVD
il DVD
eel dee-voo-DEE

CD
il CD
eel chee-DEE

CD-ROM
il CD-ROM
eel chee-DEE rohm

flash drive
la chiavetta
lah kyah-VEHT-tah

laptop
il portatile
eel pohr-TAH-tee-leh

mouse
il mouse
eel mowz

keyboard
la tastiera
lah tah-STYEH-rah

modem
il modem
eel MOH-dehm

monitor
il monitor
eel MOH-nee-tohr

router
il router
eel router

tablet
il tablet
eel TAHB-leht

printer
la stampante
lah stahm-PAHN-teh

scanner
lo scanner
loh SKAHN-nehr

to copy	**copiare**	koh-PYAH-reh		to print	**stampare**	stahm-PAH-reh
to delete	**cancellare**	kahn-chehl-LAH-reh		to save	**salvare**	sahl-VAH-reh
desktop	**il desktop**	eel desktop		to scan	**scannerizzare**	skahn-neh-ree-DZDZAH-reh
file	**il file**	eel file		screenshot	**lo screenshot**	loh screenshot
folder	**la cartella**	lah kahr-TEHL-lah		server	**il server**	eel server
offline	**offline**	offline		software	**il software**	eel software
online	**online**	online		to undo	**annullare**	ahn-nool-LAH-reh
password	**la password**	lah password		virus	**il virus**	eel VEE-roos

at
chiocciola
KYOH-chchyo-lah

hash
cancelletto
kahn-chehl-LEHT-toh

percent
percento
pehr-CHEHN-toh

circumflex
accento circonflesso
ah-CHCHEHN-toh
cheer-kohn-
FLEHS-soh

ampersand
E commerciale
eh kohm-mehr-
CHYAH-leh

asterisk
asterisco
ahs-teh-REE-skoh

tilde
tilde
TEEL-deh

tab key
il tasto Tab / il tabulatore
eel TAHS-toh tahb / eel tah-boo-
lah-TOH-reh

caps lock key
il blocco maiuscole
eel BLOK-koh mah-YOOS-
koh-leh

shift key
il tasto maiuscolo
eel TAHS-toh mah-YOOS-koh-loh

ctrl (control) key
il tasto ctrl
eel TAHS-toh chee-tee-
EHR-reh EHL-leh

exclamation mark
punto esclamativo
POON-toh eh-sklah-
mah-TEE-voh

alt (Alternate) key
il tasto alt
eel TAHS-toh ahlt

spacebar key
la barra spaziatrice
lah BAHR-rah
spa-tshya-TREE-cheh

minus / dash
meno / trattino
MEH-noh / traht-TEE-noh

plus
più
pyoo

equal
uguale
oo-GWAH-leh

colon
due punti
DOO-weh POON-tee

semicolon
punto e virgola
POON-toh eh VEER-goh-lah

dot / full stop
punto
POON-toh

question mark
punto interrogativo
POON-toh een-tehr-roh-gah-TEE-voh

enter key
il tasto invio
eel TAHS-toh een-VEE-yoh

forward slash
barra
BAHR-rah

back slash
la barra retroversa
lah BAHR-rah reh-troh-VEHR-sah

back space (or backspace) key
il tasto indietro
eel TAHS-toh een-DYEH-troh

delete or del key
il tasto cancella
eel TAHS-toh kahn-CEHL-lah

amusement park
il parco di divertimento
eel PAHR-koh dee dee-vehr-tee-MEHN-toh

aquarium
l'acquario
lah-KWAH-ryoh

art gallery
la galleria d'arte
lah gahl-leh-REE-yah DAHR-teh

art museum
il museo d'arte
eel moo-ZEH-oh DAHR-teh

botanical garden
l'orto botanico
LOHR-toh boh-TAH-nee-koh

cinema
il cinema
eel CHEE-neh-mah

circus
il circo
eel CHEER-koh

discotheque
la discoteca
lah dee-skoh-TEH-kah

trade fair / trade show
la fiera / il salone
lah FYEH-rah / eel sah-LOH-neh

garden
il giardino
eel jyahr-DEE-noh

night club
il night club
eel night club

opera house
il teatro dell'opera
eel teh-AH-troh dehl-LOH-peh-rah

concert hall
la sala concerti
lah SAH-lah kohn-CHEHR-tee

park
il parco
eel PAHR-koh

planetarium
il planetario
eel plah-neh-TAH-ryoh

science museum
il museo della scienza
eel moo-ZEH-oh DEHL-lah SHEHN-tsah

sights
le attrazioni
leh aht-trah-TSYOH-nee

theatre
il teatro
eel teh-AH-troh

tourist attraction
l'attrazione turistica
laht-trah-TSYOH-neh too-REE-stee-kah

water park
il parco acquatico
eel PAHR-koh ah-KWAH-tee-koh

zoo
lo zoo
lo dzoh

accordion
la fisarmonica
lah feez-ahr-MOH-nee-kah

bugle
la tromba
lah TROHM-bah

clarinet
il clarinetto
eel klah-ree-NEHT-toh

bagpipes
la cornamusa
lah kohr-nah-MOO-zah

banjo
il bangio
eel BAHN-jyoh

cymbal
i piatti
ee PYAHT-tee

castanets
le nacchere
leh NAHK-keh-reh

cello
il violoncello
eel vyoh-lohn-CHEHL-loh

drum
il tamburo
eel tahm-BOO-roh

electric guitar
la chitarra elettrica
lah kee-TAHR-rah eh-LEHT-tree-kah

flute
il flauto
eel FLOW-toh

drum set
la batteria
lah baht-teh-REE-yah

harmonica
l'armonica
lahr-MOH-nee-kah

guitar
la chitarra
lah kee-TAHR-rah

grand piano
il pianoforte a coda
eel pyah-noh-FOHR-teh ah KOH-dah

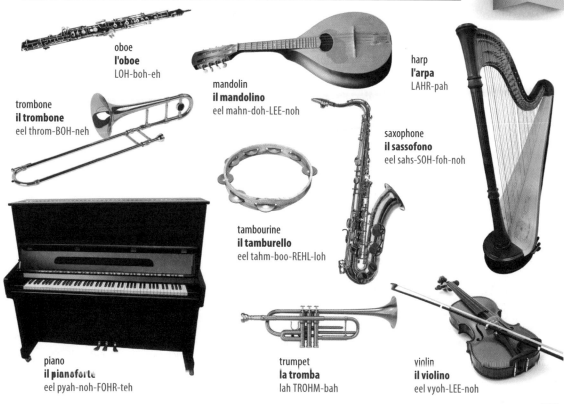

oboe
l'oboe
LOH-boh-eh

mandolin
il mandolino
eel mahn-doh-LEE-noh

harp
l'arpa
LAHR-pah

trombone
il trombone
eel throm-BOH-neh

saxophone
il sassofono
eel sahs-SOH-foh-noh

tambourine
il tamburello
eel tahm-boo-REHL-loh

piano
il pianoforte
eel pyah-noh-FOHR-teh

trumpet
la tromba
lah TROHM-bah

violin
il violino
eel vyoh-LEE-noh

Index